THE BOOK OF YOU

**DAILY MICRO-ACTIONS
FOR A HAPPIER, HEALTHIER YOU**

SMALL THINGS MATTER

We all have it in us to live a happy, healthy life!
Yet self-improvement can be difficult, and knowing
what to do on a day-to-day basis is not always
obvious or intuitive.

**Your life is the sum of the small micro-actions
you do every day, and every choice you make
is significant.**

This book will empower you to make change
happen – one micro-action at a time.

Because the small things matter.

HOW TO USE THIS BOOK

The Book of YOU makes self-improvement bite-sized. Give the book just one minute of your day, every day, and it will give you simple micro-actions you can do for a happier, healthier you.

When you've completed a micro-action, tick it off in the circle provided at the top of the page. You'll also find space to write down your thoughts and note down your achievements.

What is a micro-action?

A micro-action is small, simple and achievable in a normal day. For anyone. 'Meditate for twenty minutes' isn't a micro-action but 'sit quietly for two minutes' is. 'Run a marathon' isn't a micro-action but 'take the stairs' is. Simple, but they make all the difference.

MICRO-ACTION CATEGORIES

Each micro-action comes under one of four categories:

 FOOD: Food is such an integral part of how you live that small, simple changes in how you eat can add years to your life. 'Food' micro-actions are not only about what you eat but how, when, how much and with whom. 'Stop eating chocolate' is not a micro-action. 'Snack on a veggie' is.

 MIND: The mind determines who you are and how you act. But it isn't set in stone – it can be trained. 'Mind' micro-actions tackle mindfulness (being present in the moment), productivity and organization (making sense of the world around us). 'Tidy the house' is not a micro-action. 'Organize the kitchen cupboard' is.

 MOVE: 'Move' micro-actions are about everyday movement – small, easy micro-actions that you can incorporate into your daily routine. 'Sign up for a triathlon' is not a micro-action. 'Do two minutes of heel kicks' is.

 LOVE: Don't be fooled by the title – it's not about romance. 'Love' micro-actions are about your relationship with yourself and others. Here, micro-actions really matter. Treating someone well triggers a positive reaction in that person, which triggers a positive reaction in you too. 'Make a new friend' is not a micro-action. 'Reach out to someone' is.

HOW DO I START?

There are 365 micro-actions in this book: one for each day of the year. We suggest you start at number 1, then after the first few you can either follow the daily order or jump around to mix things up – it's completely up to you.

HOW DO I MAKE THE MOST OF IT?

• **Take your time** – Change works most effectively in small steps, so don't try to over-achieve. Take your time, and reflect on each micro-action.

• **Be open** – Be open to different micro-actions, but if the micro-action is just not for you, simply turn to a different page and perhaps come back to it another day.

• **Repeat micro-actions** – The key to creating lasting change is to form new habits. Having a habit means your brain does it on autopilot, and it can last you a lifetime. Many habits can be formed in around 28 days, so use the 'Reflect and Renew' pages to record and follow up on them.

• **Make it your own** – We're all different, so make this book work for you. Write in it. Doodle in it. Carry it around as a companion. Flip through the pages. Skip micro-actions. Redo micro-actions. Do it alone, or with your loved ones.

Get ready to start living a happier, healthier life, for you.

THE BACK STORY

The Book of YOU was born out of an app called YOU-app.
We at YOU-app have always been passionate about
health and personal change, and the road here has
been an interesting one.

We know that change is hard for most people.
We all make big resolutions and struggle to fulfil them.
In fact, 9 out of 10 fail, resulting in us feeling worse
about ourselves.

We've been there. We've struggled with the same issues
as most people – finding that elusive 'work-life balance',
feeding your body right, a healthy self-image and not
getting bogged down in the stresses of everyday life.

We wanted a simpler approach. We started working
on micro-actions because science, as well as our own
experiences, has proved it's the small changes that
truly make a difference. Micro-actions build the habit
of success, and behaving just a bit differently inspires
more awareness and personal progress.

And so, YOU-app was born. The movement of
YOU is about the power of small changes to have
a real impact on your life. We want to bring a sound,
fresh voice to the diet-crazy, transformation-obsessed
world of self-improvement.

WHO WE ARE

YOU is a team effort. The team consists of designers, developers, micro-action creators, the marketing team and the brilliantly warm and supportive YOU community.

Former management consultant turned eager entrepreneur, **Nora Rosendahl** is the editorial engine behind the YOU micro-actions. Engineer by background and with years of experience solving tough business problems for some of the world's largest companies, she's often the odd one out in the health start-up scene. A meditative weekend spent in self-reflection changed the course of her career, and Nora now combines creative writing, empathetic community management and hard-core number crunching on a daily basis for YOU.

Engineer by background, entrepreneur through passion and musician at heart, **Nelli Lähteenmäki** is a true people connector. An interest in sales took her to San Francisco, a passion for growth entrepreneurship made her stay and a longing to build a health start-up made her return to Finland and start the journey that eventually led to YOU. A bundle of positive energy and with a network to die for, Nelli can navigate any start-up scene like a lioness on the savannah plains.

With a determined, thoughtful and decisive touch, **Aleksi Hoffman** steers the direction of the YOU product. He has a background in engineering and bioelectronics, so can be trusted to code anything from healthcare IT to IPTV systems. A passion for personal behaviour change, a visual eye to match any professional designer, a heart of gold and a perfect overhead squatting technique make Aleksi a solid rock to lean on.

The designing duo other teams would kill for, **Jaakko Hyvärinen** and **Toni Sallinen** are the powerhouse behind the YOU brand and visual identity. With a creative touch, crazy humour and a human-centric approach they carefully craft the YOU we know and love.

And it's not just us, we've made some good company along the way. Among others, we've enlisted the help of category-specific experts, such as Jamie Oliver and Caroline Arnold. You can find out more about all of our guest contributors on the next few pages.

Now we're on a mission to make the world healthier and happier, one micro-action at a time.

CONTRIBUTOR BIOGRAPHIES

Jamie Oliver (Food)

Jamie's micro-actions exist to help everyone eat better and have a healthier relationship with food, one step at a time. After refocusing on his own health over the last two years, YOU-app has provided a powerful platform for Jamie to offer up his in-depth food knowledge, as well as tips he learnt during a recent qualification in nutrition. Jamie is a global phenomenon in food and food campaigning. Over a sixteen-year television and publishing career, he has inspired millions of people to enjoy cooking from scratch and eating fresh, delicious food.

Caroline Arnold (Mind)
Caroline is the author of Small Move, Big Change: Using Microresolutions to Transform Your Life Permanently. As well as being an advisor for the YOU-app and an international speaker on how to exploit the dynamics of personal change to achieve permanent self-improvement, Caroline is also a managing director at Goldman Sachs in New York.

Dr Tara Swart (Mind)
Dr Swart is an Oxford-trained medical doctor who worked in psychiatry for seven years, has a PhD in neuroscience and started up a brain-based leadership consultancy in 2008. She is the author of two books, as well as a global speaker on sustainable behaviour change and resilience.

Darya Rose (Food)
Darya is the author of Foodist and creator of Summer Tomato, one of TIME's 50 Best Websites. She received her PhD in neuroscience from UCSF and her bachelor's degree in Molecular and Cell Biology from UC Berkeley. Darya spends most of her time thinking and writing about food, health and science.

Dani Stevens (Move)

Dani believes in starting small but dreaming big. In her ten-year journey to fitness and wellbeing, she has lost close to 100 kilograms over the course of four pregnancies. A busy mum, she proves that you don't need an army of fitness trainers and private chefs to turn the dream of enjoying a healthy lifestyle into reality. As a Fitness Food Motivator DaniStevens.com has a community of over 200,000 people across the globe.

Jamie Sawyer (Move)

Jamie is one of the UK's leading strength and conditioning coaches and is also a personal trainer. His experience has taken him from working with elite athletes to Hollywood A-listers. Jamie uses his knowledge of sports science to create bespoke training, nutrition and lifestyle regimes.

1. **USING THE BOOK OF YOU**

Making the decision to live happily and healthily is the crucial first step towards changing your life for the better.

Use The Book of YOU in the way that suits you best – on your nightstand as a daily diary to record your micro-actions and thoughts; as a 'coffee table book' to give you occasional inspiration; or carry it around with you to reach for when you have a spare minute. So today, simply reflect on how best to make time for you every day and what you hope to achieve from this book.

....

....

....

....

....

....

....

2. **THANK A PERSON WHO MAKES YOU HAPPY**

Having positive people around you gives you energy
and a more positive outlook on life. Take a moment to reflect
on someone you love who's a positive force in your life.
How could you show your thanks to them?

3. **LET'S GET PHYSICAL**

You don't have to climb mountains, pound treadmills or
lift weights to get active. Research shows that just working
small, extra movement into your day has amazing health
benefits. Make a regular journey more physical – park at
the far end of the car park or climb the stairs instead of
using the escalator. Whatever it is, no matter how big
or small, just get moving more. **Jamie S**

4. **TAKE A MOMENT**

Take a moment without any disturbances to simply observe your surroundings. When life feels busy we often forget to take the 'me time' that our minds need to relax, refresh and regroup. Do you regularly take time during the day to pause? Observe your surroundings for 5 minutes.

5. **FILL YOUR FRUIT BOWL**

Today, stock up your fruit bowl, and if you don't have one –
get one! I like to think of fruit as nature's sweet shop – it's
delicious, pretty much the simplest snack there is, and of
course it's all packed with different and wonderful vitamins,
minerals and nutrients. To see snacking on fruit as a pleasure
not a chore, just stack up your fruit bowl with lots of lovely,
colourful, seasonal choices. **Jamie**

6. **YOUR COMMANDMENTS**

Why not devise some personal commandments?
Today, take a moment to think about what's important
to you and create three personal commandments –
for example, 'Keep a positive outlook' or 'Put family first'.

Record them here:

....

....

....

....

....

....

....

7. **TAKE CARE OF YOURSELF**

Neglecting personal needs can impact physical and mental wellbeing, and putting off scheduling appointments creates low-level anxiety that can dampen your productivity. Today schedule an appointment with a doctor, dentist, accountant or neglected friend. You'll feel more relaxed immediately and it only takes a phone call. **Caroline**

8. **ENJOY THE WEATHER**

All weather is beautiful in its own right. Today, take a few minutes and enjoy the weather outside, whether it's ambient rain, cheerful sunshine or a dark and stormy sky. How will you make the most of the weather?

9. **HUMBLE H$_2$O**

Being hydrated is super important as it means everything in our bodies works better – especially our brains, which are more than 70% water. Try swapping juice and fizzy drinks for H$_2$O today. The cheapest way to hydrate is to turn the tap on. Water doesn't have to be boring: get creative with natural flavour combos. Think zingy citrus slices, cucumber ribbons, fresh mint or basil leaves, juicy berries or fresh ginger. **Jamie**

10. **PICK A NEW HABIT**

Whether it's brushing your teeth, washing your hair or
putting on your make-up, habits constitute 40% of what
you do every day. They're crucial to help rest the mind.
Creating a new habit has the power to improve your health,
appearance, productivity, relationships and work life.
And the magic of a habit is that once it's been established,
it will support you for life. Decide on one micro-action you
will make a habit. Flip through the book to get inspiration
on what your next new habit could be.

11. **MAKE YOURSELF SMILE**

How are you putting a smile on your own face today?
Research shows that the mere act of smiling will actually
make you feel happier! Do it early, and your smile can
spread the mood to other people throughout the day.

12. **WORK IT IN TO WORK IT OUT**

Simply planning to exercise makes a big difference to whether you actually do it. Commit to a simple exercise routine for next week. Book it, call someone up to arrange a session, write it down – however simple it is, it will help you to make it happen. For an extra boost, lay out your gear the night before. **Jamie S**

13. **A QUICK FIX**

Today, fix something in ten minutes or less. Change a light bulb, sew a button on a shirt, install fresh batteries in a device, fertilize a plant. Repair just one thing. These tasks may not be critical, but completing one will make you feel back on top of things. **Caroline**

14. **PRACTISE MINDFUL EATING**

Eating better is not only about what you eat but how,
so try to practise mindful eating. Think about what you're
eating and why. At your next meal, take a moment to
appreciate the sensations. **Darya**

15. **PAY SOMEONE A COMPLIMENT**

Giving and receiving praise increases goodwill and lifts mood
in both the giver and receiver. Making someone feel good is
likely to make you feel good too, putting a spring in your step.
Today, be mindful and vocal about the contributions and
positive attributes of others, and feel the boost. **Caroline**

16. **A HABIT TO HANG ON TO**

Here's a crazy fact – we make more than 200 decisions about food and drink every day and, out of those, we are aware of fewer than 15 of them. Today, identify a good eating habit that you want to keep. Becoming a bit more aware of the choices you make when it comes to food is the first step to improving your overall health. **Jamie**

17. **UNSUBSCRIBE**

Is your inbox inundated with promotions and newsletters? Today, unsubscribe from unnecessary emails. See how many mailing lists you can remove yourself from in five minutes. Searching for the word 'unsubscribe' in your inbox can help you target unwanted subscriptions. **Caroline**

18. **WRITE A SHOPPING LIST**

Sounds simple, doesn't it? But whether scribbled on the back of an envelope, tapped into your phone or written in a cute little notebook, a shopping list could save you money and mean you're less likely to impulse buy – which in turn can often mean spending too much money, buying food you don't need and ending up with food waste. Follow this simple step and take a few minutes to write a shopping list to avoid that impulse-buy cycle today. **Jamie**

19. **TWO-MINUTE WORKOUT: STEP IT UP**

Moving your body doesn't have to be hard – we have endless
possibilities around us to add a bit of extra movement to the
day, we just need to notice them. For example, use the stairs
and steps around you. Two minutes spent walking up and
down those will work up a real sweat. **Dani**

20. **MAKE A CONNECTION**

Happiness may seem like a fluffy, subjective topic, but extensive research on the science of happiness has shown that there are ten main factors that drive it. One of them is connecting to other people. Pick up the phone, send a postcard, order some flowers – connect to someone today.

21. **TAKE A REAL BREATH**

Our breathing is often too shallow. Try diaphragmatic breathing – it activates the lower parts of the lungs, which are seven times more efficient at helping our cells get in the good stuff (oxygen) and get rid of waste (carbon dioxide). This kind of breathing also has lots of other benefits: calming us down and improving stress management, digestion and blood pressure. Try it out. Place one hand on your chest and the other on your belly. Breathe in through your nose for three seconds, hold for three seconds, then exhale through your mouth for five seconds. Throughout the breathing, only the hand on your belly should move. **Jamie S**

22. **MAKE A DAILY ROUTINE INCONVENIENT**

If you build movement into your daily routine, you will ensure that you move more throughout the day – and it really adds up over time. Use a small glass so you have to get up to refill it with water more frequently, move the bin to a different place, park at the far end of the car park, take the longer way round.
Jamie S

23. **HOME EXERCISE**

We often think that being active involves spending hours at the gym, but you can achieve a healthy lifestyle much more simply. Add small micro-movements into your day. Get up and do squats over a chair, run up and down some stairs, take a walk around the house or do some work in the garden to get that blood flowing. **Dani**

24. **A CULTURAL MICRO-EXPERIENCE**

Did you know that cultural activities improve the bond
between the two halves of your brain? Anything counts –
from reading a novel to attending an opera or going to
the theatre, from visiting a gallery to writing a poem
or story, or even doodling. **Tara**

Have a go here:

FOOD

25. **A FAMILY MEAL**

Sharing scrumptious food with the people you love is one of life's great pleasures. Take the time to enjoy a home-cooked family meal today or this week. Gather your loved ones around one table – whether that's your partner, a family spanning generations or the bunch of mates you live with – and enjoy some tasty homemade grub. **Jamie**

26. **JUST FEEL IT**

Notice how you are feeling today. Blue? Excited about the week to come? Nervous, happy or hopeful? Write down a few thoughts and, if you're feeling negative, just let it go.

27. **TAKE STOCK**

Devote a bit of time today to take stock of your fridge's contents. I bet it gets to a certain point every so often when your fridge – like mine – has been totally neglected. So have a rummage and pull out all those half-used, leftover and past-their-prime items. Use them up – turn them into meals, freeze them or simply pop them at the front of the fridge so they're not forgotten. **Jamie**

28. **OFF WITH DIGITAL ALERTS**

It's hard to make progress on priorities when a beep, buzz or notification alert interrupts you every thirty seconds. This digital chain-jerking can be a real drag on productivity. Turn off one or more alerts today to regain some focus. **Caroline**

29. **FIND MICRO-MAGIC IN YOUR DAY**

Remember when you were a kid and everything around you had the potential to generate wonder and awe? Find some magic again today, be it in the sound of the rain, looking up at the moon, discovering something in nature, the laughter of a loved one or a quiet moment alone.

30.
REFLECT
AND
RENEW

As mentioned in the introduction, the most effective way to create lasting change is to create new habits. Many habits can be formed in around twenty-eight days.

Write down a few notes and feelings from the past weeks.

Do you have a favourite micro-action so far?

Now's the best time to pick one and make it your Keep It Up action for the month to come.

31. **EAT GREEN**

Today is a simple one – eat something green. We all know the green stuff is good for us. Spinach might not make us Popeye-strong but it's loaded with vitamin A, which helps us see properly, especially in the dark. Greens like broccoli, peas, kale and cabbage are packed with vitamin C, which our bodies need for pretty much anything and everything. Embrace those greens in a meal today! **Jamie**

32. **TACKLE ONE BAD EATING HABIT**

We've all got naughty habits that catch us out, so today is time to 'fess up. Identify one bad eating habit and tackle it, proactively making a healthier choice instead. You could swap a fizzy drink for naturally flavoured water, eat rather than skip brekkie, swap that 4pm sugar fix for something wholesome or just be a bit more mindful about your portion control. **Jamie**

33. **LISTEN TO A POWERFUL SONG**

Music can make us do and feel all sorts of things: feel better, run faster, smile, cry, recall a memory. So listen to a song today that is powerful to you. What does it make you do or feel?

34. **SOMEONE ELSE'S PERSPECTIVE**

Choose a person close to you – someone you may be annoyed with, have frequent quarrels with or occasionally just don't get along with. Step into their shoes for just a moment. What does life look like from where they are standing? What's important and what isn't? Try to remember what this felt like the next time you meet.

35. **EVERYDAY MICRO-MINDFULNESS**

Choose a daily habit, such as brushing your teeth, having a coffee or taking the tube, and – while doing it – simply pause and pay attention. Allow yourself to be fully in the moment. Try to make it a daily habit to be mindful in that same situation – you'll feel the difference in a matter of weeks.

36. TWO-MINUTE WORKOUT: PLANK AWAY

Focus on either a knee-supported or push-up-style
plank and see how long you can hold your position.
If you're a beginner, try a thirty-second plank four times.
If you're more advanced, hold your plank for two
minutes straight. How long can you go? **Dani**

FOOD

37. **START THE DAY RIGHT**

Breakfast is boss, so give it some love today. If you get this
right, you'll be set up for the day. The key to a winning
breakfast is to try to mix it up and eat from as many of the food
groups as possible so you get a good balance. And don't eat
the same thing every day. The ideal breakfast is packed with
a combination of wholegrains, fruits, vegetables, dairy and
protein – a great example is a bowl of porridge made with
milk, topped with fresh fruit, nuts and seeds. **Jamie**

38. **NOTICE YOUR HUNGER**

Before eating, take a moment to notice what hunger feels like in your body. Remember how wonderful it is that you get to enjoy food in order to satisfy your body's needs. Next time you're hungry, pause and appreciate the feeling of anticipation for your meal. **Darya**

39. **TWO-MINUTE WORKOUT: WALL SIT**

For this easy workout you don't even need a chair – just a wall. Slowly slide your back down a wall until your thighs are parallel to the ground. Make sure your knees are directly above your ankles and keep your back straight. Work up to holding the position for two sets of sixty seconds. **Dani**

40. **DECLUTTER IN FIVE MINUTES**

Reducing clutter helps you gain clarity and paves the way for
better routines. We all have loads of stuff we no longer need
but it can seem overwhelming to deal with a whole cupboard
or box. So open a drawer and spend five minutes choosing
just a handful of things to toss. **Caroline**

41. **BE GRATEFUL**

This micro-action can unlock vast reserves of wellbeing.
We tend to think about life in relative terms – was today
better than yesterday, am I doing better than my colleague,
where am I in relation to my goals? Be grateful. Don't dwell
on what you're lacking but be happy for what you have.

42. **TRY SOMETHING NEW**

Get adventurous today and eat an ingredient you've never tried before. Most of us buy the same stuff, week in, week out, year in, year out. So it's time to mix things up. Today, choose something – fruit, veg, cheese, fish, meat, grain or spice – you've never picked up before. Have fun! **Jamie**

FOOD

43. **CHOOSE WHOLEGRAINS**

Choose a wholegrain option today. Eating wholegrains
regularly will make a massive difference to your health – they
are powerful little things and can reduce the risk of strokes and
heart disease. Without getting too geeky, they remain whole
when they're processed, whereas refined grains lose lots of
their nutrients during milling. Also, wholegrains take longer to
digest, which helps to keep us feeling fuller for longer. I also
find that wholegrain varieties such as wholemeal bread or
brown rice give brilliant texture and often have a deeper
flavour, so they're great for adding an extra level to
your meal. Double pleasure. **Jamie**

44. **ONE-MINUTE DIARY**

Take less than a minute to write down one thing that happened today. Keeping long diary entries every day is a resolution that a lot of us fail at, so make this short and manageable. What may seem like an ordinary or insignificant moment today can become a dear memory years from now.

....

....

....

....

....

....

....

....

FOOD

45. **EAT THE RAINBOW**

Knock out a colourful meal today (but keep it natural!).
A lot of info flies around about how to get all the vitamins
and minerals you need for optimal health, wellbeing and
mood. But let's break it down: the simplest, easiest, most
effective way to ensure you're getting your fill of the good
stuff is to eat the rainbow. Different colour veggies and
fruits give us a whole range of different nutrients. The
more fresh, seasonal colour on your plate, the better,
so mix it up! **Jamie**

46. **EXPLORE THE NEIGHBOURHOOD**

Put on your walking shoes and go out to explore your surroundings. Notice something new. Find a place you haven't visited before. Admire something for a second longer than usual. When you are paying attention to what's around you and get lost in the moment you may not only experience something new but also end up walking that extra mile.

47. **TAKE QUALITY TIME**

Today, take some quality time. It may be time for yourself
doing something you love – read, write, work on a building
or gardening project. It may be for pampering yourself – have
a bath, enjoy the sun, put your feet up. Or it may be time spent
with your loved ones. Make it quality time and make it count.

48. **LIGHTEN YOUR PAPER LOAD**

Without noticing it, we tend to acquire a lot of unnecessary
things, which we then carry around. Go through your briefcase,
handbag, wallet or pockets and get rid of old papers, receipts,
extra notebooks and journals. Clearing your bag is like
clearing your mind. **Caroline**

49. **IMPROVE A HABIT**

Today is not about lofty resolutions but about improving an existing one. What habit are you trying to work on and how could you make it stick even better? Set yourself reminders, ask a friend for support, set smaller goals or invest in those cool new trainers to inspire your next workout. Whatever helps.

50. **SIT DOWN TWICE**

You may look a little odd but when sitting down today, even just at your desk or to watch TV, do it twice. We spend a lot of time sitting, which leaves our glutes underused. They are the largest muscles in our bodies and going from sitting to standing activates our glutes, quads and hamstrings. Double up: sit down twice! **Jamie S**

51. **ASSIGN A SURFACE A PURPOSE**

Surfaces are clutter magnets. We drop post, bags, keys and loose change anywhere handy. While you don't need to put everything away immediately, making sure that surfaces don't become catch-alls is important. Post doesn't belong on a kitchen island, a comb and brush aren't useful on a desk. Today, rearrange what's on one surface in your life so that it serves a specific purpose. You'll be more organized in minutes. **Caroline**

52. **FORGIVE YOURSELF**

Regrets and self-reproach can weigh you down – they don't call it 'emotional baggage' for nothing! Focus on an old regret or an old faux pas and give yourself a break – forget about it. What has passed has passed, but the future is right now. Make that future brighter – forgive yourself and move forward. **Caroline**

53. **A MEAL TO SHARE**

It's all about the love, baby! Share some food with a loved one.
Whether it's a romantic proposition or quality time with a dear
old friend, we all know that the way to someone's heart is often
through their stomach. Make the time this week to cook up
a delicious meal from scratch that you can share. **Jamie**

54. **TAKE IT ALL IN**

Take a moment to take it all in. When we're busy we often rush from one thing to the next and forget to stop and appreciate our surroundings. And that's really the easiest mindfulness exercise you can do. Take in the nature around you, appreciate your colleagues, observe your family from a distance or admire the night sky. Whatever you do – be in the moment.

55. **SHAKE IT OFF**

A happy and healthy lifestyle starts with the right attitude.
What's an old attitude you're shaking off and what are
you replacing it with? Don't hurry through this one,
make it count for you.

Write it here:

....

....

....

....

....

....

....

....

....

56. **CHECK YOUR POSTURE**

Most of us spend a lot of the day sitting, which negatively
impacts our posture. It means muscles aren't being used
in the way they were designed to. Correcting your posture
can activate and strengthen muscles that have switched off.
When you sit, sit to attention! Standing, pinch your shoulder
blades together and pull down. Try sitting with good
posture as long as possible without back support.
Walk with your head held high. **Jamie S**

57. **READ FOR FIVE MINUTES**

Picking up a book for even a few minutes is a great habit.
We love films, TV and the world of content on our smart
phones, but acknowledge that a good book is best for giving
your mind both a rest and some stimulation. Pick up a book or
magazine, relax and just read for a few minutes. How could
you make reading for five minutes a day a new habit?

FOOD

58. **STOP WHEN YOU'RE FULL**

Today, stop eating when you're full (and I'm talking full, not stuffed!). It sounds simple but a lot of us eat until we've finished everything on our plate, as opposed to when we're no longer hungry. Maybe because we still have our parents' voices ringing in our ears telling us not to leave the table until our plates are clean! Try and combat that old message today, keeping any leftovers for another meal. **Jamie**

59.
**REFLECT
AND
RENEW**

For this reflect and renew micro-action,
think about what you have learned so far.

What has been most insightful?

Which micro-action has been your favourite?

Are you ready to change your Keep It Up action?

60. **LEFT OR RIGHT?**

We can get quite stuck in our ways, always typing on our tablets with the same hand, always holding our knife and fork in the same hand, etc. Doing something with your non-dominant hand is great stimulus for your brain. So try it today: write a few sentences, eat a meal or brush your teeth. You might even find it surprisingly fun! **Tara**

61. **SHOPPING-BAG WEIGHT TRAINING**

Often it's really the small opportunities to move which are the best. When I go shopping with the kids, holding the bags becomes a bicep curl workout. Ditch the trolley, hold your shopping bags and do some bicep curls as you walk to the car. **Dani**

62. **STAND UP**

Standing is great for us and we should endeavour to minimize sitting time. So today, stand up. This is a great example of how micro becomes macro: standing for three extra hours a day, five days a week, for one year uses the same energy as running ten marathons! **Jamie S**

FOOD

63. **SIT AT THE TABLE**

We're a constantly distracted generation. How many of you
are eating while reading this book? Or usually munch brekkie
while checking emails, or grab lunch on the go or have a few
too many TV dinners? Food is one of life's simplest pleasures.
You're much more likely to overeat if your mind is elsewhere.
So sit at a table for your meals today. **Jamie**

64. **QUIETEN DOWN FOR FIVE MINUTES**

Even if you enjoy being busy, taking a quiet moment once in a while is a really good habit to get into. Put everything aside and take a few minutes to refocus. Relax. Try to do nothing and enjoy it.

65. **ACTIVATE YOUR ABS**

If you don't use it, you lose it. While you are, for example, making breakfast or on the bus, pull your belly button in. This micro-action is amazing for your lower back as it activates the deep abdominal muscles that are usually asleep but help provide support. Activate your deep abs without effort today. **Jamie S**

FOOD

66. **GET FRUITY**

Keeping it super simple, just eat some fresh fruit today.
Too many of us don't and those of us that do can easily get
stuck in a rut with what we choose. Fruit has loads of amazing
nutritional benefits, plus it's delicious and pretty much the
simplest snack there is. The more varied we keep our choices,
the more benefits we get – so mix it up and eat the rainbow.
Jamie

67. **THINK POSITIVE**

Almost everything we do starts as a thought, and each
thought impacts how we think, act and feel. Today,
take control and consciously think more positively about
something. Positive thinking accumulates – people who are
primed to think positively see more possibilities, take on
activities and develop skills a negative-thinker would not.
If you want to learn more about the power of positive
thinking, there are some amazing TED Talks on the subject.

68. **MAKE YOURSELF LAUGH**

Humour doesn't just boost your mood, it's good for the
body too. Laughing stimulates your heart, lungs and muscles,
and releases endorphins in your brain. So today, make sure
you enjoy a good laugh.

FOOD

69. **GUILTY HABITS**

Today, tackle one of those little guilty habits that can sometimes hold you back from positive change. We've all got them, whether it's going in for an extra helping or sneaking another biscuit from the tin when you think no one's looking. Which of your guilty pleasures can you tackle today? Perhaps you're a breakfast-skipper or a kids-dinner-finisher. Be bold, and make a change. **Jamie**

70. **REACH OUT TO SOMEONE**

We all have those friends or relatives we've wanted to call for a long time. How about seizing the moment and reaching out to them today? Grab the phone, write a message, pay them a visit, send them a gift or just text a smiley face.

71. **LEAVE YOURSELF A NOTE**

Write a positive or uplifting note to yourself for tonight. Leave it on the fridge, the kitchen table or ready to be found when you go to bed. If you can't think of anything to say to yourself, leave a note for someone else!

72. **MODIFY ONE MORNING HABIT**

Mornings can be a hassle. Take some time today to run through your current morning routine in your mind. What's working and what isn't? Find one thing you could improve in the mornings. For example, pick up the habit of reading the news, add in five minutes of meditation, prepare your clothes the night before or simply leave home ten minutes earlier.

73. **TWO-MINUTE WORKOUT: WALL SQUATS**

Find a wall, face it and stand approximately thirty centimetres away. Place your hands behind your head, bend down slowly and do as many squats as you can in two minutes. How many can you do? **Dani**

74. **THE TWO-MINUTE RULE**

Quite simply, if something takes two minutes or less to complete, do it right away. Don't write it down, don't add it to your to-do list, just do it. It's surprising how many simple things we put off when we could get them done really quickly.

75. **BOOK BREAKFAST WITH A FRIEND**

When life gets busy with family, work or studying we often struggle to find enough time for friends. Mornings are a great time to meet as the day's tasks have yet to begin, so call up a friend and make a breakfast date.

76. **DECIDE WHAT WON'T GET DONE TODAY**

Many of us start each day with the assumption that we can get
everything on our to-do list completed. As a result, we don't
decide early enough what to put off and by the end of the day
the choice has been made for us. Start today by deciding what
won't get done, then focus like crazy on your shortlist. Part of
mastering productivity is accepting the limits of your day
and making conscious choices – before the day slips away.

Caroline

77. **TAKE A WALK**

Try taking short walks during the day to shake it up.
A two-minute walk in the office every twenty minutes can
be surprisingly beneficial for your health – research even
shows it can be more beneficial than an hour at the gym
after work! So get up, get out and take a short walk.
For an added challenge, do not take your phone.

78. **BEAUTIFUL FRESH HERBS**

Today, use some fresh herbs in a dish. I've said before
that if herbs didn't exist I'd probably give up cooking!
They really are a complete joy and are key to taking any
meal to the next level. Each one does its own incredible
thing and the more you experiment the more amazing
combinations you'll discover. Woody herbs, such as
rosemary, thyme and sage, are brilliant with meat and
in the base of heartier dishes, and softer herbs, such
as mint, basil, parsley and coriander, are great in
salads, pastas, for sprinkling over dishes or even
for making your own pesto. **Jamie**

79. **WHAT DO YOU LIKE ABOUT YOURSELF?**

We often spend so much time focusing on the small things
we're lacking or what we think is wrong that we forget
to see the good. Especially when it comes to ourselves.
Take a moment and write down one thing you really like
about yourself. Whether it's a physical attribute, a skill
you have or a strength – we all have something to be
proud of on a daily basis.

....

....

....

....

....

....

....

....

80. **GET READY FOR BED EARLY**

Get ready for bed well before bedtime. Wash your face, floss
your teeth, soak your contacts, recharge your phone. Get it all
done early so that as soon as you feel tired you can go straight
to bed without having to do a single thing. **Caroline**

81. **RETRO WALKING**

Most commonly known as 'backwards walking', this originated
in ancient China, where it was practised for good health.
When you walk backwards, it puts less strain on your knee
joints, making it ideal for people with knee problems or injuries.
Also, because backwards walking eliminates the typical heel
strike to the ground (the toe contacts the ground first), it can
lead to changes in pelvis alignment and help to open up the
facet joints in your spine, potentially alleviating lower back
pain in some people. So go backwards! **Dani**

82. **EAT SEASONALLY**

Eating bang-in-season veg and fruit means you get it at its best – it's super fresh, at its tastiest and at its cheapest too. Check out a calendar of seasonal foods, get inspired and take your pick. Use one seasonal veg or fruit in a meal today. **Jamie**

83. **FEEL AN EMOTION**

To create sustainable change you need to get engaged
emotionally as well as logically. The basic eight emotions
are: fear, anger, disgust, shame, sadness, joy/excitement,
love/trust and surprise. You can use these to get yourself
more or less engaged in an activity. Today, think how you
can use one of these feelings to your advantage. **Tara**

84. **SHARE SOMETHING THAT MAKES YOU LAUGH**

Found a funny picture on the internet? Or did you
just hear a great joke? Share it with a friend today.
Sharing is caring and laughing is loving.

85. **MAKE A SUSTAINABLE CHOICE**

Make one green choice that shows the natural world some love. Here are a few ideas: opt out from paper junk mail or move to paperless billing. Get a reusable water bottle (30 million water bottles are produced annually, and only 20% get recycled). Reuse your plastic bags (3 trillion are used globally each year, and only 6% are recycled).

86. **PREP ONE THING FOR TOMORROW**

At any point during today, prepare one thing for tomorrow. Lay out your clothes, pack your backpack, prepare your lunch or jump-start your breakfast. Whatever you prepare tonight will allow you to sleep a little longer and begin your day with less stress. Tomorrow morning is going to be a breeze. **Caroline**

FOOD

87. **LOVE YOUR FREEZER**

Show your freezer some love. What I mean is, make the most
of it! Your freezer is your best mate when it comes to saving
waste and keeping healthy stuff in stock. One of my favourite
things to do is chop up fruit on the turn, bag it up in portions
and freeze it ready to whiz up as smoothies. Buying frozen veg
is also brilliant – the veg is often frozen really swiftly after
it's picked so nutrient-wise it's all still happening. Also you
can just use what you need, when you need it. **Jamie**

88.
REFLECT
AND
RENEW

Use this moment as motivation to renew your
commitments to yourself, particularly
your favourite micro-actions.

89. **GO PAPERLESS FOR ONE NEW BILL**

Have you been meaning to switch from paper bills to e-bills but can just never find the time? Today, select one monthly bill you receive in the post and opt for electronic billing instead. The environment, your post box and your sanity will thank you for it.
Caroline

90. **FIND AN OLD PICTURE OF YOUR FAMILY**

Do you have a box of photos from the days when pictures were still taken on film, developed and printed on paper? Today, take a trip down memory lane and sort through your old family photos. Pick your favourite and let it remind you of days gone by.

91. **PLAN A WEEKEND ACTIVITY**

Make the most of an upcoming weekend by doing something
active. Plan something like going for a hike, for a walk or going
shopping on foot. Feeling frisky? Plan an adventure! No time?
Commit to ten push-ups on Saturday morning to get you going.

92. **CONCENTRATE ON LUNCH**

Take thirty minutes to enjoy your lunch away from phone,
email and other interruptions and you'll likely have a more
productive afternoon. The break will allow you to savour
your meal, consider afternoon priorities and end your
day with greater vigour. **Caroline**

93. **COOK FROM SCRATCH**

If you cook from scratch and use lovely fresh ingredients,
you essentially have your health in your own hands. Cook a
meal from scratch today. Knowing how to cook is an essential
life skill. For any kitchen novices out there, a few simple recipes
up your sleeve will serve you well for a lifetime, so get your
cookbooks out or get online and find a recipe that inspires
you to get in the kitchen. **Jamie**

....

....

....

....

....

94. **DO A TASK YOU'VE BEEN PUTTING OFF**

Select one task languishing on your to-do list. Pick up that extension lead at the DIY shop, change the hard-to-reach light bulb in that cupboard, call an elderly relative, make an appointment to get your teeth checked. Just pick one thing from your nagging to-do list and get it done today. **Caroline**

95. **SLOW THE BEAT**

Play music with a slow beat during mealtimes. You'll naturally tend to eat with the rhythm, so slow down and eat more mindfully by playing soft music. **Darya**

96. **TAKE A STRETCHING BREAK**

Interrupt whatever you are doing and stretch. One minute
is enough. Stretch your arms, legs, back, neck. Even a quick
mobilization is good for both body and mind. **Jamie S**

97. **READ SOMETHING NEW**

Teachers encourage children to read a lot to help instil the
'story structure' so they learn to think in sequence while their
brain still has a lot of plasticity. For adult brains, reading
something new can improve your creativity – so if you love
novels, maybe go for non-fiction or even poetry today,
or try to learn something new. **Tara**

FOOD

98. **PRIDE OF PLACE**

If you're surrounded by beautiful, tempting fresh options, you're more likely to put them in your mouth! Move the good stuff to pride of place today. In my house we always have a well-stocked fruit bowl close to hand, give a big bowl of salad pride of place on the dinner table and have jugs of water in the fridge chilled and ready to pour. Get shuffling! **Jamie**

99. **LEARN A PLACE ON THE MAP**

Knowing where places are not only improves your worldly
wisdom but learning keeps your brain active. Take a few
minutes to study a map. Learn at least one new place.
Can you pin-point Ljubljana? The capital of Tibet? Kuopio?

100. **DROP SOME EMOTIONAL BAGGAGE**

Give up an old grudge, forgive a friend or colleague for
something, stop dwelling on an old regret or apologize to
someone you've treated unfairly. Old emotional business
weighs you down – they don't call it 'baggage' for nothing.
Today, target some old business and forgive, forget
and move forward. **Caroline**

101. **WORK AROUND THE HOUSE**

Do a few small tasks that take you around the house. We all
have those little things we know we should fix, improve, start
or finalize – and ticking things off our to-do list can help get
us moving too. Is it a leaking tap, a light bulb that needs
changing, a plant that needs watering or that pile of leaves
in the garden you could gather up? Put on your work boots
and complete a few small tasks that get you physical.

102. **IMPROVE YOUR SLEEP ENVIRONMENT**

Sleep is when your brain rests. It's when your muscles relax
and develop. It's also when you replenish your energy stores
to take on the world again the next day. What small
improvement could you make to your sleep environment
to ensure a better night's sleep?

103. **YOUR POSITIVE MANTRA**

We spend much of our time fretting about the negatives instead of focusing on the positives. Get in front of the mirror today and tell your reflection a positive mantra. For example: 'Happiness isn't size-specific', 'Work out because you love your body, not because you hate it' or 'I am strong, I am beautiful, I am enough'. What are you telling yourself today?

104. **CLEAN UP ONE THING**

Wipe down the fridge, straighten a corner of your desk, clean the keyboard on your laptop, return stray items to the medicine cabinet. It's amazing how five minutes of clean-up can change your entire outlook and make life feel manageable again.

Caroline

105. **A CHILDHOOD FOOD HABIT**

The earlier we learn good food habits the better – good habits
learned young make for a healthier, happier life. Think back
and identify one of the good food habits you picked up as a
child. Was it a meal you learned to cook that you still knock out
today? Perhaps you were nagged about eating your greens
and it's stuck? Whatever it is, celebrate that positive habit
and keep it up! **Jamie**

106. **GO NUTS**

Today, pay homage to the wonderful world of nuts.
They're incredible – deliciously diverse in flavour, packed
with beneficial unsaturated fats and lots of essential vitamins
and minerals, and will give you an energy boost. Try just
a small handful as a snack or added to a meal – pecans
on porridge, pine nuts over pasta or crushed walnuts over
a salad. And if nuts won't do, a sprinkle of seeds is also
a really good way to go. **Jamie**

107. **DELEGATE ONE THING**

One key to greater productivity is delegation. Most of us take on too much and only think of delegating when it's too late. Today, identify one item you can delegate. It might be a duty for an upcoming social event, asking someone at work to write up the key points of a meeting or getting your child to set the table. Delegating is a skill. It takes practice to learn how to spot a delegable item and get it on to someone else's to-do list before it's too late. **Caroline**

108. **GO TO SLEEP FIFTEEN MINUTES EARLIER**

There is no greater productivity boost than sleep. Sleep restores your willpower, decision-making and active initiative resources. Sleep rebalances hormones for steady energy. Sleep allows your subconscious to make new connections and discoveries that will support your problem-solving. Even just fifteen minutes more sleep can make a big difference.
Caroline

109. **WALK AN EXTRA MILE**

One mile is approximately 1.6 kilometres and about 2,000 steps. Could you get off the bus a stop or two earlier, park the car further away, add in an after-lunch walk, take your phone calls while pacing around or resolve to always walk up the stairs? Try to achieve it one or more days this week. Small changes really do add up over time. **Jamie S**

110. **FIND KINDNESS AROUND YOU**

The science behind how witnessing happiness can affect our wellbeing is fascinating. Today, stop, look around and notice small acts of kindness. Is it a person, item, service or moment? Where can you find kindness today? Can't find it? Create it.

111. **FRUIT SWITCH**

I can't bang on enough about fruit – it's nature's genius way of making it easy to get the good stuff into your diet. Today, switch up your usual fruit choice. Whether you have a banana at brekkie, grab an apple at 11am, or blitz up the same smoothie combo each morning, challenge yourself today to choose a fruit you don't usually pick. Each fruit has a different nutritional makeup, so mixing things up will do your body a favour, as well as being a treat for the tastebuds. Choose something seasonal so it's at its tastiest and best! **Jamie**

112. **PARK BENCH OR CHAIR STEP-UP**

Find opportunities outside or at home to do small bursts
of movement. Here's a simple one: when you are out and
about and spot a bench, or in your home with a chair,
do step-ups. Step up with one foot, then the other and
repeat fifteen times on each foot. This will tone your
legs and get your heart pumping. **Dani**

113. **EAT WITH GRATITUDE**

Take a few seconds before you eat to remember all the
people and resources that went into creating your meal.
Appreciate the farmers, the soil, the sunshine, the water,
the shops and, yes, yourself as well. **Darya**

114. **MAKE SOMEONE ELSE SMILE**

Spread the joy by making someone else smile. Everyone feels lonely at times, so try to think of someone who might need some cheering up – be that a loved one or a complete stranger. The reward centre of the brain actually gets a stronger dopamine hit when we make someone else smile first.

115. **READ ONE PIECE OF NEWS**

Do you know what's happening in the world? In your home country or town? Open a news site, skim through and read at least one full article. Reading the news helps you gain perspective and can take your mind off your own challenges.

116.
REFLECT
AND
RENEW

In this review, write a short eulogy for yourself.

Reflecting on what you want to be remembered
for can increase your level of happiness and give
you perspective on life.

Does your vision fit with the person you are today?

117. **GET CREATIVE WITH VEG**

We all have a repertoire of dishes we bang out, week in,
week out, but mixing things up and getting inspired with new
recipe ideas is crucial to keeping veg on your menu long term.
Today, get creative with veg. Switch up salads by using
a speed peeler to add ribbons of courgettes and carrots,
or grate a load of gorgeous fresh veg to make a slaw.
Use your imagination and have fun! **Jamie**

118. **VOLUNTEER FOR SOMETHING**

Volunteering is a great way to help those in need around you. You'll feel great too, for doing something that really matters. So help out a friend, volunteer to carry your neighbour's shopping up the stairs or do some research into volunteering opportunities close to you.

119. **TWO-MINUTE WORKOUT: EVENING STRETCH**

Take two minutes to truly stand silent and listen to your breathing, then start with some light stretches to get your muscles moving and your blood flowing. Our seated or standing positions throughout the day can tense up our muscles, and those tensions need to be released. **Dani**

120. **BE A TOURIST IN YOUR HOME TOWN**

Travelling expands our thinking and gives us perspective.
But why not get the same effect without leaving your own town?
There are a lot of new things to experience and see if you look
through the eyes of a tourist. Go out today and explore.

121. **TAKE A WALK AT LUNCH**

Walking for just eight minutes can improve creativity
and problem-solving for hours afterwards. A brisk walk
after lunch will also boost your metabolism and prevent
that mid-afternoon slump that can hit us both in the
workplace and at home. **Caroline**

122. **CREATE A DREAM PAGE**

Dream boards are a great way to visualize your aspirations.
Fill this page, or use the space below, with writing and doodles
to make them concrete. This is a great escape when you need
it, and making things visual may just give you that little extra
nudge you need to pursue what you wish for.

123. **KEEP YOUR WATER BOTTLE OR GLASS FILLED**

Water boosts brain function and physical stamina, and helps keep ideas and energy flowing all day. The trick to drinking more is simply to always have water within reach. Practise keeping your glass filled all day today. **Caroline**

124. **MEASURE MINDFULLY**

We have lots of ways to measure ourselves. Many people weigh themselves, count their calories consumed, hours slept, steps walked, etc. – but it can become obsessive. So cut back on counting and measure only one or a few things that really matter. Or just listen to your body. Be mindful of how you feel and whether you need a rest. **Jamie S**

125. **NOTICE AN ANIMAL, TREE OR FLOWER**

Nature is amazing, but we rarely notice just how amazing.
Watch a documentary or, even better, go outside and
explore nature. Find a flower, a tree or an animal
and look up its name.

126. **LEARN ONE THING ABOUT HOW YOUR BODY WORKS**

Knowing how the body works is key to making it work better
for you. So open a dictionary or a book or browse some reliable
websites and learn about the human body. What interesting
fact can you find that helps you treat your body better?

127. **GET-AHEAD GRUB**

Today, prepare one thing to save you time and stress over the next few days. You could try cooking a big batch of super-healthy grains to toss through lunchbox salads, or freeze portions of fruit ready to blitz up an easy breakfast smoothie. I love to get a big pot on the stove and make a hearty ragu to toss through pasta, have on toast or freeze for a lasagne. What can you do to make meals a little bit easier this week? **Jamie**

128. **COMPLIMENT A STRANGER**

Have you ever had a stranger on the street compliment your
outfit or your looks? Did you get an endorphin rush that lasted
for the rest of the day? Make it your mission to compliment
a stranger today. It may be a complete stranger on the bus
for something they're wearing, the barista at your favourite
café for his or her coffee-making skills, or that stylish older
gentleman living next door to you. There's a guaranteed
good feeling for you too.

129. **LISTEN TO CLASSICAL MUSIC**

Classical music has been shown to reduce blood pressure,
reduce stress and anxiety, and improve sleep quality. Put on
some classical tunes and unwind. What are you listening to?

130. **SUBJECT MATTERS**

We all have at least one topic we're knowledgeable about.
Be it history, Japanese gardening, mathematical theories, the
Second World War or parenting techniques – it's your game.
What is your favourite subject? Today, consider how you
can better cultivate that knowledge in your daily life.

131. **MOVE TOGETHER**

Moving together keeps you more accountable and makes
it more fun. Team up with a friend for a light jog in the park,
schedule a joint workout with your significant other or join
a group class. If you have kids, make your joint time active –
go walking, skating, surfing, cycling or visit the park. **Dani**

132. **ENJOY A SMALL ACHIEVEMENT**

Research has shown that it's small, frequent boosts of joy
that lead to happiness, not the rare big stuff. It's the little
things in daily life that have the power to make lasting
improvements to our happiness. So celebrate a small
achievement today – having your favourite lunch, moving
for just five minutes, choosing a book instead of your
iPad or receiving a smile from someone you like.

133. **SAY THANK YOU**

Say thank you to someone today. Two such simple
words that we often forget. Do you remember an occasion
where someone thanked you and how good that felt?
Thank someone – a friend, a colleague, a family member
or simply someone working at your local supermarket.

FOOD

134. **SNACK SMART**

Today's micro-action is to eat a clever, tasty, healthy snack that will spank your taste buds and subdue hunger. People often ask me if snacking is good or bad – well, let me clarify that snacking is absolutely good. It helps keep your blood sugar levels in check, which means you stay alert and active. But it's got to be the good stuff – I'm talking fruit, nuts, seeds, a little salad, something nice and nutritious rather than diving into the biscuit tin. **Jamie**

135. **SHOW LOCAL SOME LOVE**

Get out in your local area and appreciate your surroundings.
Find a street you haven't walked down before, nose
around some independent shops or admire the buildings
around you. Try to look at your neighbourhood as if
seeing it for the first time.

136. **ALLOW TIME FOR BOREDOM**

In a world of constant stimulation, we flip channels incessantly,
immediately pick up our phone when we're alone, always have
the TV or radio on in the background. But boredom can really
be a stimulus for change. In fact, studies show that boredom
boosts creativity as it motivates us to approach new and
rewarding activities. So today – give boredom a chance!

FOOD

137. **FIFTY SHADES OF GREEN**

Go one step further with 'eating green' today and make half of one meal green veg. The more varied you make your greenage the better, and it doesn't have to be a chore – you can sneak greens into all sorts of dishes. Think adding a handful of peas to rice, stirring spinach into mash or adding a dollop of homemade guacamole to a meal. Upping your greens will help your body tick over nicely. (Even green chillies are packed with vitamin C, which is music to my ears!) **Jamie**

138. **WHAT DID YOU ACCOMPLISH TODAY?**

Take a moment and look back on today. What did you accomplish? Write down something that felt good and why.

....

....

....

....

....

....

....

....

....

....

139. **SIT WITH YOUR TEA OR COFFEE**

Make your drink of choice, then sit down for a few minutes.
No phone, no paper, just sit and think about your week.
Source physical energy from your drink and mental
energy from a moment of stillness.

140. **TWO-MINUTE WORKOUT: PELVIC FLOOR**

Pelvic-floor muscle exercises are important for both men
and women, and are very useful to prevent incontinence,
particularly for women who have had children. Sit, stand
or lie down with your legs slightly apart and relax your thighs,
buttocks and abdomen muscles. Tighten the muscles around
your front and back passages, drawing the pelvic-floor muscles
up inside. Develop this into a daily habit by doing it while you
are stirring your dinner, brushing your teeth or about to go
to bed. Consistency is key. **Dani**

141. **PREP ONE THING**

'Failing to plan means you plan to fail' – so the saying goes.
At some point today, prep something for a meal for tomorrow.
It doesn't matter whether it's popping some meat or fish in
a marinade overnight, making an extra portion of your
evening meal ready for tomorrow's lunch, or soaking some
oats for a bircher muesli in the morning. A little bit of planning
can save you time, stress and money – enjoy. **Jamie**

142. **GET VITAMIN D – GO OUTSIDE!**

Sunshine – how we love it. It's the best source of vitamin D, which is produced when sunlight hits the skin. So get outside to fuel up – and why not take a brisk walk while you're at it!

143. **SET A TECH RULE**

Technology brings us many wonderful things, but it can be a distraction from real life and deep down many of us know we're a bit addicted. So today, set a clear tech timeout rule. No phones or TV at the dinner table? No digital devices after 9pm? Only checking email once per hour? Turning off all alerts when you leave the office? Write down your chosen rule here:

....

....

144. **SIT AND ENJOY A MEAL**

Walking or driving while eating can make it feel like you
aren't having a meal at all. And research confirms that you're
more likely to overeat when you're distracted by another task.
Take the time to sit down and really savour your food today.
You deserve it. **Darya**

145. **SET A GO-TO-SLEEP ALARM**

We use alarm clocks to get us up in the morning, but for many
the challenge is actually the night before – going to bed early
enough. So try this. Decide on a bedtime (count seven to eight
hours back from your wake-up time) and set an alarm for
when it's time to go to sleep.

146.
REFLECT AND RENEW

Today, reflect on what type of micro-actions work best for you.

Recall an instance when you've really felt that a micro-action has positively impacted your day and consider why that was.

Have you repeated that micro-action yet?

If not, today's the day to do so!

147. **BALANCED BREKKIE**

I'm sure we've all heard over and over that breakfast is the most important meal of the day and let me tell you, it really is! Show breakfast the love it deserves and eat a balanced brekkie today. Make it a joy, not a chore – try pimping your porridge with a sprinkling of cinnamon, whizzing up a beautiful berry smoothie or cracking out some eggs. Whatever you do, enjoy it! **Jamie**

148. **A STRENGTH OF YOURS**

What's one thing you're really good at? Take a moment
of reflection and write it down. It may be your ability to
think positively, your 'can do' attitude, effective working
practices, a magically intuitive empathy or your brilliant
analytical skills. Whatever your strengths are, identifying
them makes you more likely to actively use them,
and hence strengthen them even further!

149. **ONE ROOM DECOR**

Decorating your home is rewarding work, but may feel like
a huge chore. Pick one room in your home (or just one part of
one room) and address that. Shift around the placement
of furniture, add a fun new item, play around with different
colours or simply rearrange a bookshelf to look nice.

FOOD

150. **USE UP ONE THING**

In the UK we throw out 4.2 million tonnes of edible food every year. That seems crazy to me, so today get food smart and do your bit to help reduce that massive figure. Use up one food item that was destined for the bin. If you've got bread that's seen softer days, tear it up and bake it to make croutons or blitz it into breadcrumbs for sprinkling on a pasta dish. Create a lovely jumbled-up chopped salad from odds and ends in your veg drawer or simply chuck some fruit in the freezer ready to stew up for an easy dessert. **Jamie**

FOOD

151. **HEALTHY HEART**

To keep our hearts nice and healthy, it's important to keep our intake of saturated fat below 20g a day. Do one thing today to reduce your saturated-fat intake. I often swap the butter on my toast for avocado (I love butter, but everything in moderation).

What can you do? Here are a few tips: measure oil with a measuring spoon to give you more control over the amount you use, trim away the excess fat from meat or skim away any fat that rises to the top of meaty stews. You can also grill, poach, boil, steam or bake food – and, my favourite, use yoghurt instead of cream wherever possible. **Jamie**

152. **ENJOY AN INSPIRATION**

Get inspired. Trigger new thoughts. Let your mind wander.
Think outside the box. What inspires you? Music, art,
a teacher, a book or your mother's words of wisdom?
Choose an inspiration of yours and enjoy it.

153. **GOOD ADVICE YOU'VE RECEIVED**

Recall one piece of good advice you've received in the
past. Something that made you stop and think, changed how
you look at life or at a specific problem. Was it an instant
'Eureka!' moment or did the advice inspire you over a longer
period of time? Share it today and maybe you can help
someone else in return.

154. **TELL SOMEONE YOU LOVE THEM**

Putting our feelings into words and expressing them
to our loved ones is something many of us struggle with.
But don't take love for granted – reminding the loved
ones in your life (and yourself) that you love them by
saying so not only makes you and them feel good,
but will strengthen the bond between you. Today,
tell someone in your life that you love them.

155. **STOCK UP ON ONE SUPPLY**

Zero in on a staple supply that you often run out of at
the last minute and stock up on it now. Toilet paper, cat food,
printer paper, ink or light bulbs. Either pop to the shops or
go online – get a little bit ahead on supplies and watch
your stress level decline. **Caroline**

156. **FRIDAY PREP FOR NEXT WEEK**

What's one thing you can do on Friday that's going to make Monday easier? Fill the car up with petrol? Iron an outfit ready for work? Get a load of washing done? Stock up on lunch items? Think of one thing that trips you up on Monday morning and prepare for it this Friday. You'll enjoy the weekend more and you'll have more energy next week if you take care of it in advance. **Caroline**

157. **WEAR WHAT MAKES YOU FEEL GOOD**

What you wear can have a really big impact on your mood, self-image and confidence. Put a little extra effort into what you wear today and choose clothes that make you feel really good. Be it that new dress, a smart suit, warm woollen socks or your favourite old T-shirt.

158. **TWO-MINUTE WORKOUT: BURPEES**

Burpees are one of the most effective full-body exercises around. Try and bust out as many burpees as you can to lift your heart rate. This is an excellent two-minute morning workout to get the day started. Don't know what a burpee is? Look up a tutorial video online. **Dani**

159. **SKIP A COMPLAINT**

At some point today, you may be tempted to complain – about the weather, travel, a family member or office politics. Instead of giving in to sounding off, see what it does for your mind and spirit just to let the moment pass without comment.

160. **TAKE A 'THINKING TEN'**

Tackling your to-do list day after day puts the brain in
'execution' mode. That's great, but make sure you are doing
the right things. Take a 'Thinking 10' today and reflect on
your priorities for ten minutes.

....

....

....

....

....

....

....

....

....

....

161. **IT'S A WRAP**

One thing we can all do to minimize waste generated by food is to cut down on packaging. Don't worry if you aren't a keen composter or your kitchen is stuffed with carrier bags. Today, just remember to recycle or, even better, reuse one piece of food packaging. Keep a houmous pot to pack snacks for on the go, use plastic bags as bin liners or, if you want to go really green, use an empty tin as a pot to grow fresh herbs on your windowsill! **Jamie**

162. **REMEMBER A WOMAN IN YOUR LIFE**

Think of a woman who has had a big impact on you –
it can be someone who has been important at some point
in your life, or someone that you see every day – and extend
your appreciation to them. Call, send a message or write
a letter to them; it will surely make their day.

163. **CHECK YOUR PHONE ONLY EVERY HALF-HOUR**

The fight for mental real estate is fierce. We're constantly
assaulted by beeps, pop-ups, vibrations and advertisements.
When we get into a meeting, we check our phone. When
we're cooking dinner, we stop to check our phone. We can't
control the environment, but we can control ourselves. Limit
yourself to phone checks only every half-hour and see
what it does for your productivity. **Caroline**

164. **ONE EASY SWAP**

Today, swap one piece of food or drink for a healthier choice. We've all been there, made a vow to drastically change our eating habits and found ourselves face-first in the fridge at 10pm. So instead of giving something up, just swap it out for a more nutritious option. The more realistic your habit changes are, the better chance they'll stick. **Jamie**

165. **TAKE A CAT NAP**

A five- to ten-minute nap in the afternoon works wonders on productivity for the rest of the day. The trick is finding a quiet and cosy place to take that nap. If you're at home, it's easy; at work, perhaps a little tricky. But with practice, you can learn to sleep almost anywhere. Set the timer on your phone and close your eyes. Even if you don't fall fully asleep, when you open your eyes you'll be refreshed. **Caroline**

FOOD

166. **SHOW-STOPPING SPICES**

Cooking from scratch with spices will elevate your cooking to
the next level and help you make it sing. Experiment with some
new spices today. The right combo can turn a simple dish into
something really special. They're also a really clever way to
lower your salt intake as they are so packed with flavour,
you can often get away with using less seasoning. **Jamie**

167. **SURGERY-FREE EYEBROW LIFTS**

Moving your face is like moving your body – it relaxes and tones muscles. For two minutes, lift your brows up and down (and try not to laugh too much). This exercise lifts and improves the shape of the brows: it reduces frown ridges and lines in between, opens up the eye area and lifts the upper eyelid, reducing hooded and wrinkled eyes. The increased tone in the muscles over the scalp gives a general lifted effect to the forehead! **Dani**

168. **HELP OUT IN YOUR COMMUNITY**

To make a difference in the world we often think about global causes and lofty goals, but there are lots of opportunities to do this much closer to home. Find a cause in your own community where you can help out. Be it planting some flowers in a community garden, volunteering for a non-profit organization or helping your neighbour. Every act of kindness counts.

169. **WHAT'S BEST RIGHT NOW?**

On any given day, no matter what else might happen, there's
always something positive to appreciate. It may be a situation,
a feeling, something you did well, a kind word or an event
you're looking forward to. What's best right now for you?

Write it down here:

FOOD

170. **QUICK KITCHEN CLEAR-UP**

Today, de-clutter one kitchen surface or cupboard. It doesn't have to be a proper deep clean, and no elbow grease will be needed. Just pick one area of your kitchen that hoards the most clutter and be brutal. Take no prisoners – banish anything that has nothing to do with cooking. (I'm looking at you, piggy banks and magazine racks!) Having your kitchen kit close to hand and not surrounded by clutter will help you to be more instinctive and efficient in the kitchen. **Jamie**

171. **TWO-MINUTE WORKOUT: HEEL KICKS**

To elevate your heart rate or bust a cardio workout, kick
your heels up to your bottom and go hard for 30 seconds,
then rest for 10 seconds. Do this three times for a quick
cardio session. **Dani**

172. **A CULTURAL EXPERIENCE**

Book tickets to the theatre, make a plan to visit a museum,
admire architecture or pick up a classic book. This is soup for
the soul. Cultural activities have been linked to increased
wellbeing, so get out there and get cultural!

173.
REFLECT AND RENEW

Take a moment to celebrate the things that you've accomplished while working through this book.

Be honestly proud of how far you have come!

Then look ahead – what do you want to achieve before the end of the book?

Try to break that goal down into small micro-actions for the next phase.

174. **TEN-MINUTE 'FUTURE DREAMING'**

For ten minutes, sit down in a quiet place and do some
'future dreaming'. No need to make any grandiose plans,
just let your thoughts drift to a nice vision of the future.
Where will you be, with whom, doing what? What could
you do today to get you closer to that vision?

Write some ideas down here:

FOOD

175. **SNACK ON A VEGGIE**

Keep it simple and snack on a veggie. Vegetables are
the unsung heroes of the snack world – they feature heavily
at lunch and dinner, but are often kept on the snack sidelines.
It's pretty easy for bad snacking habits to slip under the
radar – even the most saintly of eaters can fall victim to that
4pm sugar-fix snack attack. So today, when you need a
pick-me-up between meals, reach for a veggie. **Jamie**

176. **TIDY UP**

Keeping order can be as simple as straightening things up a little bit, often. Today, try to do this every time you leave a room – whether it's the kitchen, the garage or your desk/office at work – tidy something up. Put a stray book back on the shelf, smooth out a pile of papers, sweep coins off a bureau and into your wallet. You'll be surprised at the difference it makes to your surroundings and your mood. **Caroline**

177. **TWO-MINUTE WORKOUT: COUCH DIPS**

When an ad break comes on, while watching TV, take advantage of the pause to do sets of dips on the couch or a chair. This is a great tricep workout that will help to tone your arms where they wobble. **Dani**

178. **A MEMORY-FILLED SONG**

Music has amazing powers. It can stimulate old memories as vividly as if they happened yesterday. Take a trip down memory lane and listen to a song that reminds you of a person, situation or beloved place.

179. **COOK FROM SCRATCH**

If you cook from scratch and use lovely fresh ingredients, you essentially have your health in your own hands. Cook a meal from scratch today. Knowing how to cook is an essential life skill. For any kitchen novices out there, a few simple recipes up your sleeve will serve you well for a lifetime, so get your cookbooks out or get online, and find a recipe that inspires you to get into the kitchen. **Jamie**

180. **EVERYONE LOVES A MISFIT**

Most supermarkets reject fruit and veg that isn't perfect –
20% to 40% is wasted in the UK alone. Today is all about
embracing unusual fruit and veg to support our farmers.
The natural stuff comes in all different shapes and sizes
and is just as delicious and nutritious no matter how it looks.
Get creative and show your support to save waste.

181. **ORGANIZE ONE SHELF**

Open your bathroom cabinet, pick one shelf, remove things
that don't belong, wipe down the shelf and reorganize the
remaining items – all in five minutes. Organizing just one shelf
is fast, easy and immediately reduces clutter. **Caroline**

182. **COSY UP AT HOME**

Today, curl up in a blanket with a book, have a mug of hot chocolate, lounge around on colourful pillows or watch your favourite film to cheer you up! What is 'cosy' to you?

183. **CONQUER A CRAVING**

Focus in on a craving for eating something naughty and satisfy it with a more wholesome choice. Life would be a boring place if we didn't indulge in tasty treats every now and again, but cravings can often get the better of us. For instance, instead of mid-afternoon choccie, freeze some grapes to snack on or swap that one-coffee-too-many for a therapeutic herbal tea. **Jamie**

FOOD

184. COOK DON'T CHUCK

Save a sad ingredient from being thrown away and use it in a meal. Got a few carrots nudging towards softness? Make a soup. There's a really geeky satisfaction that comes with using up food that would've otherwise been chucked, and you're helping the planet too. **Jamie**

185. **SEEK OUT FEEDBACK**

Today, ask a colleague, family member or friend for feedback.
Seeking out feedback at work inspires thoughtful responses
and boosts your standing by demonstrating that you are
dedicated to performing to the best of your ability. Asking
a friend, partner or family member how you might improve
your approach to something creates trust and can give
you new personal insight. To improve, you don't have
to agree, just listen. **Caroline**

You might find it helpful to record the feedback here:

....

....

....

....

....

....

....

186. **PLAY WITH A BALL**

For today's workout, find your inner child and do something
involving a ball. Play tennis, juggle, play fetch with a dog,
challenge someone to a football game or just play catch
against the wall by yourself. Enjoy! **Jamie S**

187. **A PHRASE IN A FOREIGN LANGUAGE**

Learning new languages is one of the best ways to increase
your brain's neuroplasticity as an adult. Today, flex the
language centres of your brain and learn a useful phrase
in another language. If there is a place you've always wanted
to go, learn to say 'thank you' in that country's language.

188. **ENJOY THE MOMENT**

We tend to rush through routines, chores and to-dos, always
focusing on the next thing on our agenda. This can be good for
getting things done, but we run the risk of forgetting to enjoy
the moment. So today, pause and be present in what you're
doing. It could be taking time over your morning tea or coffee,
finding something funny or relaxing with your feet up in the
evening. What moment will you fully enjoy today?

....

....

....

....

....

....

....

189. **REACH OUT TO SOMEONE**

We all have those friends or relatives we've wanted to call
for a long time. Now is a better time than ever to reach out.
Grab the phone, write a message, pay them a visit, send
them a gift or just text them a smiley face.

190. **A SONG YOU DANCE TO**

Today, play a song that makes you dance. You may be
someone who can break out into dance at any appropriate
(or inappropriate) moment, someone who dances alone while
vacuuming or a dedicated party dancer. Whoever you are,
there's always that song that will get you grooving –
so put it on and get on down!

191. **PUT YOUR TO-DO LIST LAST**

End your day today by making tomorrow's to-do list.
This will help you put into perspective what you need
to get done, and provide a visual reminder of your
priorities first thing in the morning. **Caroline**

Write your own to-do list here:

....

....

....

....

....

....

....

....

192. **MAKE A MEAT-FREE MEAL**

Us humans eat a lot of meat and it's a huge drain on the environment. It takes more than 15,000 litres of water to produce just two beef steaks, compared to under 300 litres to produce 1 kilogram of potatoes – that's a big difference! Today, enjoy a meat-free meal. As well as being good for the environment, celebrating veggies will probably save you a bit of cash too. **Jamie**

193. **COMPLIMENT YOURSELF**

Every thought and emotion creates a neurochemical reaction
that affects your wellbeing. Today, say a few words of
affirmation to yourself. What have you achieved recently
that you're proud of? What do you like when you look
in the mirror? Complimenting yourself gives confidence,
balance and a positive spin to the day.

194. **WHAT CALMS YOU DOWN?**

We all have our own ways of managing stress, of relaxing and refocusing. What calms you down? Becoming aware of the most effective way for you to calm down is an important first step to start doing it more consciously and regularly.

195. **MAKE YOUR BED**

The simple act of making your bed in the morning can combat the blues. This may sound strange, but it starts the day off on the right track, gives a visual lift to the room and makes it more inviting to go to bed in the evening when the sheets aren't all crumpled up from the night before. Try to make it a habit to make your bed – it only takes two minutes.

196. **ENJOY SILENCE**

Take a moment and enjoy the silence. If you live in a city,
you're probably surrounded by noise most of the time, but even
outside the city we tend to fill up silences with different sounds
such as TV, music or radio. Make a conscious effort to find
a silent place and enjoy the lack of sound. Just give your
mind the space to run free and fill the void itself.

197. **FAVE FRUIT**

Today is about celebrating gorgeous, seasonal, tasty, fresh
fruit! Simply eat your favourite fruit. They all contain different
vitamins, minerals and nutrients, which help keep our bodies
healthy, so a good philosophy to remember going forward
is to eat the rainbow and mix up your choices! **Jamie**

198. **ASK SOMEONE FOR ADVICE**

Nothing builds a bridge like asking someone for their opinion or counsel, and getting someone else's perspective can help you make better decisions. Today, think about something you've been trying to solve by yourself and seek out someone's advice. Thinking of refinancing but don't know how to compare options? Wondering if you should seek flexible working hours at work? Reaching out to a personal or professional connection for a conversation will not only help you solve a problem, it will strengthen a relationship that could prove invaluable.

What advice did you receive?

....

....

....

....

....

....

FOOD

199. **POWER UP WITH PLANT PROTEIN**

Meat and dairy are excellent sources of protein but let's not underestimate the power in plants! Today, eat some protein-rich nuts, seeds or grains, such as quinoa. Some pulses are great plant protein sources too – think lovely beans, lentils and chickpeas. Protein is mega important – we need it for growth, muscle repair and brain function. **Jamie**

200. **A DISTANT MEMORY**

Take a moment to recall a distant memory. The memory is a powerful tool – by sitting down and recollecting, you can resurrect strong emotions and thoughts. Recalling good memories vividly helps boost your overall happiness. So take a trip down memory lane to a positive event in your past.

201. **DO SOMETHING SILLY**

We can easily get into the macro-habit of taking life way too seriously. Small acts of silliness are the best cure – today, do something genuinely silly. Jump into a big puddle of water, climb a tree, play a prank or challenge someone to a wrestle.

REFLECT
AND
RENEW

Use this review to make a list of five fun things
you want to do in the next few months!

Be it to make homemade pasta, learn how to paint,
head off on a get-away with a friend or learn
how to whistle – just make it fun.

203. **TWO-MINUTE WORKOUT: SUPERMAN UP AND AWAY!**

We all want some superpowers, right? Lie face down with
arms and legs extended. Keeping the torso as still as possible,
simultaneously raise the arms and legs to form a small curve
in the body. Do this ten times, rest and repeat. **Dani**

204. **QUIETEN DOWN FOR FIVE MINUTES**

Even if you enjoy being busy, taking a quiet moment
once in a while is a really good habit to get into.
Put away the phone and take a few minutes to refocus.
Relax. Try to do nothing and enjoy it.

205. **COIN COLLECTION**

Take ten minutes and collect all the loose change you can find – from your bag, your wallet, your dresser and out of your coat pockets. Sort it, total it and put it into bags marked with the amount – and then spend it. It feels like free money and you'll be happier without all that loose change rattling around. **Caroline**

206. **TWO-MINUTE WORKOUT: SQUAT WHILE YOU DO**

Not only does squatting get your glutes toned but your core and legs too. Record how many squats you can do in two minutes, then try to beat your score each time. This is also great for multi-tasking. For example, are you brushing your teeth or waiting for the kettle to boil, or even waiting for the bus? Squat while you do. **Dani**

207. SOMETHING YOU LIKE ABOUT SOMEONE

Choose a person close to you and identify one thing about them that makes them special. Be it a personal trait, a skill or a passion, everyone has something that makes them unique. What is it for that person? Write it down and – for the best effect – tell them you appreciate it.

....

....

....

....

....

....

....

....

208. **A RELAXING SONG**

Music has been shown to have great powers over the human mind. One of them is the ability to get us relaxed. Listen to a relaxing song. Lie down. Unwind. Let your thoughts drift. You'll soon feel rested and at ease.

209. **TWO-MINUTE WORKOUT: STEP IT UP**

Moving your body doesn't have to be hard – we have endless possibilities around us to add a bit of extra movement to the day, we just need to notice them. For example, use the stairs and steps around you. Two minutes spent walking up and down those will work up a real sweat. **Dani**

210. **PAUSE MINDFULLY**

Use a natural pause to practise some mindfulness. Don't wait impatiently for the green man at the traffic crossing – use this as a chance to stop, breathe and look around. Or if you're standing in a queue, or waiting for the kettle to boil or at the bus stop, just appreciate the moment.

211. **CELEBRATE COLOUR**

We've all heard that blue makes you calm, yellow is the colour of happiness, etc. The science on the psychology of colour can be fluffy, but many of us still perceive its powers. So today, wear something colourful: add a splash of colour to your home or office, find some colour in nature or put colour on your plate. You could choose your favourite colour, one to reflect your mood, or the best brain stimulus – try one you wouldn't normally choose and see how it makes you feel! **Tara**

212. **READ A POEM**

Reading poetry affects the brain in many of the same ways music does – it stimulates emotional and memory-related areas. Are you a poetry rookie? Give it a try today – you've got nothing to lose.

FOOD

213. **FOOD, GLORIOUS FOOD**

You know I'm bonkers about food, and I want you to be too.
For me, enjoying a delicious meal, made from scratch, with my
family, is the most beautiful thing. Simply appreciate your food
today. It could be a particularly mouth-watering ingredient,
the place you're eating in, the people you're with or the
whole shebang! Simple, wonderful stuff. Enjoy. **Jamie**

214. **SPOT A BEAUTIFUL BUILDING**

When we walk down the street we tend to keep our eyes fixed either on the ground, on the ad-filled window displays or, even worse, glued to our smartphone screens – and we neglect to look up. When walking down a familiar street, look up and pay attention to the buildings. Take in the splendour of your neighbourhood architecture and try to select the most beautiful building you see today.

215. **IMPROVE YOUR SLEEP ENVIRONMENT**

Sleep is one of the most important factors for our health, but it's one of the first things we skimp on when work, family life or entertainment take over. Better sleep is connected to weight loss, stress reduction and improved physical performance. So buy a new pillow, make your bedroom darker, use a different alarm clock or cool down the room. Whatever will get you to snooze better.

216. **GIVE A BOOK TO A FRIEND**

Good books are like portable magic and we often have very
personal relationships with our favourite books. Today, pick
one book to give to a friend who you think might enjoy it.
Discussing it later will not only deepen your bond but may
provide new insights and new dimensions to the book
that you have never thought about yourself.

217. **A PASSION OF YOURS**

What is a topic you feel really passionate about? We all
have one (or a few) things that make our eyes twinkle, our
minds start racing with ideas and our excitement levels build
up or that simply make us happy when we think about them.
Be it gardening, base-jumping, cooking, work, fashion or
collecting old car parts – spend a moment today reflecting
on what it is for you and what you are doing to make it
a good part of your life.

218. **TWO-MINUTE WORKOUT: SQUAT-TASTIC**

The gluteus maximus is the biggest muscle in your body and it burns energy very quickly. Squats are a great way to activate your glutes and get your blood pumping. Rattle out ten squats – anytime, anywhere – to give yourself an energy boost. **Jamie S**

219. **DRESS TO IMPRESS**

What we wear can give us a major confidence boost. Today, wear something that you really like and that makes you look really good. Look good – feel great!

220. **HOW DO YOU FEEL TODAY?**

Be honest. How do you feel today? Worried, inspired,
excited, happy, expectant, confused?

Write it down here and take a moment to reflect
on why you feel that way:

....

....

....

....

....

....

....

....

....

221. **VISIT A HIGH PLACE**

Today, climb, ride or walk up to a high place. Not only is
this a great way to exercise but you may also get the chance
to appreciate a stunning or interesting view. Use this as an
opportunity to spend some time reflecting on your day.

222. **A CHILDHOOD FOOD HABIT**

The earlier we learn good food habits the better – good habits
learned young make for a healthier, happier life. Think back
and identify one of the good food habits you picked up as a
child. Was it a meal you learned to cook that you still knock
out today? Perhaps you were nagged about eating your
greens and it's stuck? Whatever it is, celebrate that
positive habit and keep it up! **Jamie**

223. **TAKE A MICRO-BREAK**

Today, take a micro-break during the day. 'Take a break!'
is not a popular thing to say to anyone who's really busy, but
even a brief timeout will actually make you more productive
overall. What does a micro-break look like for you today? Is it a
cup of tea alone, a walk around the office, taking a moment to
look out of the window or simply turning your face to the sun?

224. **MORNING STRETCH**

After a night in bed, stretching is one of the best gifts you can
give your body. Gently wake up your muscles and joints –
stretch your arms, back and legs first thing – and keep yourself
flexible. One minute is enough, and a great habit to get into.

225. **THE MAGIC OF TOUCH**

Really tuning into our sense of touch can be one of the most amazing ways to practise mindfulness. Have you ever really stopped to think about how the fresh air feels on your skin? How real leather can feel both soft and rough? How a loved one's skin feels to the touch? Or how it feels to experience the warmth of a fire? Take a moment to mindfully tune into your sense of touch.

226. **DO SOMETHING YOU LOVED AS A KID**

Your memory is a very strong tool. Recalling good memories is
great for boosting your mood and happiness. The more details,
the better. So take a moment to recall your childhood joys.
And, even better, try to relive it!

....

....

....

....

....

....

....

....

....

....

227. **REARRANGE YOUR APPS**

What's front and centre on your mobile phone screen
determines your phone habits and can affect your productivity.
Move the most important features and apps to your home
screen and arrange the apps you use less (or think you should
use less!) in folders. You'll be surprised to find how easy
access reduces stress and helps you to maintain focus.
Caroline

228. **READ A WEBSITE RELATED TO YOUR JOB**

Take five minutes to explore a website related to your
job or hobby. There could be interesting research on an
industry website, new ideas on a competitor site or news and
postings you weren't aware of. Keeping up-to-date with what's
happening in your area will help generate new ideas –
a core productivity activity. **Caroline**

229.
REFLECT
AND
RENEW

Along any journey there are always rough patches.

Look back on the last year and identify one instance when you felt like you failed, couldn't go on, had let yourself or someone else down.

Reflect on that situation and forgive yourself.

It's what's ahead that matters.

FOOD

230. **EPIC EGGS**

Inside each eggshell is an impressive nutritional arsenal.
The humble egg is packed with protein and two eggs will provide
you with a source of a whopping eleven different vitamins and
minerals! Make eggs part of a meal today. It still boggles my
mind how affordable they are and how many quick meals you
can make with eggs so, whether you fry, poach, scramble, boil
or bash out a frittata or omelette, get cracking! Just remember
to choose free-range or organic if you can. **Jamie**

231. **EAT LUNCH AWAY FROM YOUR DESK**

Take thirty minutes to enjoy your lunch away from phone,
email and other interruptions and you'll be likely to have
a more productive afternoon. The break will allow you to
savour your meal, consider afternoon priorities and come
back to work with renewed focus. **Caroline**

232. **YOUR FAVOURITE MICRO-ACTION**

Which micro-action has been your favourite so far?
Take a moment to reflect on yours, record it here and repeat it.

....

....

....

233. **CLOSE YOUR EYES FOR A MINUTE**

Don't overthink your breaks. This time, just close your eyes
for one minute. Block out what's happening around you
and let your thoughts drift.

234. **TWO-MINUTE WORKOUT: LOW-SQUAT SITTING**

Isometric exercises (holding a position) can be a pain in the
butt (literally), but they are great for building up your strength.
The low-squat position is actually the natural resting position
for us humans, and it's a great way to open up the hip area.
So, adopt the low-squat position and hold! See if you can
keep going for five minutes. **Jamie S**

235. **A RANDOM ACT OF KINDNESS**

Kindness makes us feel good – that's clear. But did you know
that kindness is also linked to happiness and health on a
biochemical level? Kindness causes the release of oxytocin
and dopamine in the brain, which contribute to reducing
inflammation in the body and can slow the ageing process.
Who could you show a random act of kindness to today?

236. **YOUR PRODUCTIVITY TIP**

Productivity means efficiency (doing things faster or better),
but above all effectiveness (doing only the right things).
What helps you do your best work? How do you save time
in your daily routine? How do you prioritize a long to-do list?
Be creative, be practical and inspire others with one
productivity tip that really works for you.

237. **JAZZ UP YOUR BREAKFAST**

Add a healthy twist to your breakfast today. Getting a good
dose of nutrients under your belt in the morning will really
set you up for the day ahead. So jazz up your breakfast with
a nutrient-packed twist. Add fresh fruit to your porridge,
have a dollop of natural yoghurt on your cereal, swap butter
for avocado on your toast or choose poached eggs over
fried. The key to keeping up good habits is to enjoy them,
so have fun and see what works for you. **Jamie**

238. **STIMULATE YOUR SENSES**

Today, really engage your senses. Walk barefoot,
eat a piece of dark chocolate, watch the sunset,
listen to the sea, try out some perfumes ...
whatever you choose, enjoy it.

239. **BE MEDIOCRE – PROUDLY!**

It's wonderful to be brilliant at something. Most of the time, however, we're pretty mediocre. And that's good – if we accept it! Today, practise some self-acceptance and celebrate the mediocre. Enjoy a really normal moment in your life, just as it is. Self-acceptance is an important driver for happiness and functioning well. Be perfectly imperfect and proud of it.

240. **MAKE A SEASONAL FILE**

You don't need to design a comprehensive filing system to be organized – one key file can make all the difference. This file labeled for the season will collect all those loose papers you need to keep for a while but not for ever, such as receipts and bills. Put event tickets and holiday plans in the file, or an invite to a friend's party. When the season rolls around next year, go through the file and toss everything that's out of date. Easy and effective! **Caroline**

241. **SET THE TONE FOR THE WEEK**

'Start as you mean to go on' is a great mantra.
So today, set the tone for the week to come. Put a positive
spin on a problem, start the morning with a lovely breakfast,
complete a few small to-dos, decide on one important thing
you will get done or simply smile brightly at someone.
What will your week look like?

....

....

....

....

....

....

....

....

242. **TWO-MINUTE WORKOUT: HOPPING**

Stand on one leg, hop for ten counts, then swap legs and repeat. Single-leg exercises engage smaller muscles in ways we can't duplicate when training both legs together. This translates into more balanced growth and development. **Dani**

243. **FINISH EATING BY 8PM TONIGHT**

How does not eating late at night help improve productivity? You'll sleep better if you don't have a load of food to digest in your belly, and a good night's rest leads to a happier, more productive day. You'll also be more likely to eat a real breakfast tomorrow morning, setting you up for steady energy all day. One small change, many benefits. **Caroline**

244. **FAVE FRUIT**

Today is about celebrating gorgeous, seasonal, tasty, fresh
fruit! Simply eat your favourite fruit. They all contain different
vitamins, minerals and nutrients, which help keep our bodies
healthy, so a good philosophy to remember going forwards
is to eat the rainbow and mix up your choices. **Jamie**

245. **FIVE-MINUTE WORKOUT: VIRTUAL BIKE RIDING**

It's time to ride your virtual bicycle. Lie down with knees bent
and hands behind your head. With your knees in towards your
chest, bring your right elbow towards the left knee as the right
leg straightens. Continue alternating sides (like you're
pedalling). Just leave your helmet in the wardrobe :-). **Dani**

246. **TASTE IT**

For this micro-action, we'll turn food into a mindful moment.
We often rush through our meals. It's natural when we're in
a hurry, but we even tend to rush through the meals we really
enjoy. Today, when you eat, pick one thing you will really savour.
For example, take a tomato and cut it into pieces. What's
the texture; where do you feel the taste in your mouth; is it
sweeter or more savoury than other tomatoes; how do the
seeds, skin and pulp feel and taste? How long can you
enjoy that one tomato?

247. **DEFINE A REWARD FOR AN UNPLEASANT TASK**

No one wants to get down and dirty with unpleasant tasks.
Motivate yourself with a nice reward. It can be a piece of
chocolate, a bubble bath or whatever puts a smile on your
face. Then do the task and get the reward!

248. **DRAW OR DOODLE SOMETHING**

Use this space to draw or doodle something small. How about the view out of the window, an object you see near you, a cartoon or something you used to draw as a child? Don't worry about accuracy – the important thing is to let your creative side flow!

249. **DON'T DO SOMETHING**

Pick one thing you do habitually that hampers your productivity
and give it a rest today. Your not-to-do item on this list might
be 'don't interrupt', 'don't put myself down', 'don't click on
trashy celebrity stories' or 'don't shop on the internet'. See how
you feel after you don't do it for one day. You'll be surprised
how twenty-four hours gives you a new perspective. **Caroline**

250. **GOOD ADVICE YOU'VE RECEIVED**

Recall one piece of good advice you've received in the past.
Something that made you stop and think, changed how you
look at life or at a specific problem. Was it an instant 'Eureka!'
moment or did the advice inspire you over a longer period
of time? Share it today and maybe you can help
someone else in return.

....

....

....

....

....

....

....

....

....

251. **TACKLE A DIFFICULT CONVERSATION**

Whether it's a phone call you've been dreading or an
uncomfortable work discussion, deferring a difficult
conversation will depress your productivity all day. Tackle
it first thing and see your output soar afterwards. **Caroline**

252. **ENJOY A PUT-DOWN-FREE DAY**

Putting yourself and others down creates an atmosphere
of negativity that can depress you and dampen productivity.
For today, keep it all positive! Don't gossip about a friend,
dismiss a colleague's idea or tell your children that their friends
have better manners. And be kind to yourself, too – say only
positive things about yourself for twenty-four hours. Feel your
can-do coming on? **Caroline**

253. **TWO-MINUTE WORKOUT: KNEE LIFTS**

Standing with your feet hip-width apart, lift one leg up towards your chest as high as you can and lower it back down to the ground. Repeat with your other leg. Standing knee lifts are great for boosting strength in your mid-section as they don't isolate the abdominal muscles in the way that standard crunches do. Instead, they work your abs in conjunction with other key muscles. **Dani**

254. **ACT HOW YOU WANT TO FEEL**

The link between mind and body is tremendous. Today, make your body act the way you want to feel. When you feel tired your posture worsens, but this is true in the reverse as well. Smile and you'll feel happier. Stand in a power position and you'll feel more confident. Physically reach out to someone and you'll feel more connected. Acting on this insight can truly be one of the greatest changes in your life.

255. **DREAM AWAY**

Today, take a moment to daydream. Studies have demonstrated that the brain solves tough problems in the background while daydreaming. So those brilliant ideas or epiphany moments don't just 'come to you', they are the by-product of unconscious mental activity when your brain is resting. Feed your brain by giving it some downtime and daydream away.

256. **LONG-DISTANCE LOVING**

Sometimes we've all got to be reminded to do something nice
for someone we love who's not always around – whether it's
your mum, dad, auntie, mentor or your best friend who's moved
out of town. Today, surprise someone you don't often see
and remind them how much you love them and why.

257. **CLEAN A SURFACE**

Today, at home or at work, zero in on an appliance, cupboard,
light fixture, shelf, table or windowsill that's not on your
sponge's daily circuit and give it a minute of cleaning.
It will give the whole room a lift and prove that finding
time just means finding a minute. **Caroline**

258. **PREPARE A SNACK**

To tackle the snack attack, pack or prep a healthy snack.
We've all been there, caught off guard by hunger pangs
and impulsively grabbing the nearest (often not-so-healthy!)
nibble. So today, get ahead and be ready for the snack
attack – throw a small handful of nuts and dried fruit in
a tub, pack some crunchy veg sticks with a little pot of
houmous or simply pop an apple in your bag before
you head out of the door. **Jamie**

**REFLECT
AND
RENEW**

Take a moment to reflect on the micro-actions
you've undertaken over the last month.

What have you achieved?

About which areas of your life are you
feeling particularly positive?

Are there things you feel you can improve on?

260. **RUN UP THE STAIRS**

Today, ban the lift and use the stairs. Stepping is a great way to get the heart pumping, especially on the way into work, before and after lunch, and on the way home. Use the stairs today for that extra energy burst. Try to find a place where you can run up at least five flights of stairs. **Jamie S**

261. **EXTEND YOUR NETWORK**

Building networks increases productivity by enabling us to access advice, referrals and admin shortcuts. Visit the desk of a colleague or ask a fledgling connection out for quick cup of coffee. It only takes ten minutes to build a bridge. **Caroline**

262. **TECH TIMEOUT**

Deep down, many of us know we're a bit addicted to technology and too contactable. For your own benefit, it's good to draw some clear tech rules. How will you take a tech timeout today and what are your tech timeout rules?

263. **SMILE AT A STRANGER**

Has someone ever suddenly smiled at you on a busy street? Do you remember the feeling after the initial surprise? Today, when you are out and about, smile at a stranger. Not only will smiling make you feel happier, you will feel more confident for reaching out to others.

264. **EAT GREEN**

Today is a simple one – eat something green. We all know the green stuff is good for us. Spinach might not make us Popeye-strong but it's loaded with vitamin A, which helps us see properly, especially in the dark. Greens like broccoli, peas, kale and cabbage are packed with vitamin C, which our bodies need for pretty much anything and everything. Embrace those greens in a meal today! **Jamie**

265. **GIVE SOMEONE A GIFT**

Have you ever received a small gift unexpectedly? How did that feel? No need to wait for birthdays, Christmas or anniversaries – the best time to give a gift is today. It doesn't need to be big – send a postcard, pick up some flowers, get those favourite chocolates or simply do something you know will make another person happy.

266. **SET YOUR ALARM CLOCK FOR AN EARLIER START**

Today, set your alarm clock thirty minutes earlier for tomorrow.
Plan one thing you'll do in the morning with that extra time.
Will you read, take a walk, use the time for creative writing
or maybe just sit on the balcony and admire the view?
These micro-pockets of 'extra' time can sometimes
be the most valuable.

267. **A GREEN MO(VE)MENT**

Put on your walking shoes and head out. Combine a moment
of natural wonderment with some light exercise. What does
nature look like where you are and how are you making
the most of it? You don't need much – just five minutes of
'green exercise' can improve your mood and self-esteem.

268. **TRY A NEW THING**

We often get stuck in our routines and, while routines give great structure to the day, it's good to mix things up occasionally and explore the new. So cycle along a different route, try a new sport, shop for food in a new place, wear a colour you usually don't, sign up to learn something new, test a new type of tea or simply try looking at the world in a different way. Try one new thing today.

269. **BOOK BREAKFAST WITH A FRIEND**

When life gets busy with family, work or studying, we often
struggle to find enough time for friends. Mornings are a
great time to meet up as the day's tasks have yet to begin,
so call up a friend and make a breakfast date.

270. **BANISH THE MONDAY BLUES**

Come Monday morning, many of us feel the 'Monday blues'.
Don't let them define your week! Today, do, experience,
think of or invent something to cheer you up and banish
those Monday blues.

271. **ENJOY SILENCE**

Take a moment and enjoy the silence. If you live in a city,
you're probably surrounded by noise most of the time, but even
outside the city we tend to fill up silences with different sounds
such as TV, music or radio. Make a conscious effort to find
a silent place and enjoy the lack of sound. Just give your
mind the space to run free and fill the void itself.

272. **PLATE IT**

It's easy to lose track of food and eat mindlessly when you're
eating directly out of a bag or box. For both meals and snacks
it helps to see exactly how much you will be eating before you
start, which creates a natural boundary to how much you eat.
Put everything you eat on to a plate before enjoying it. **Darya**

273. **FIND BEAUTY AROUND YOU**

Take a moment to notice the beauty all around you.
There's beauty on every street corner, in every home and
office cubicle, and in that person sitting opposite you.
Focus on the moment and give it your full attention.

274. **ENJOY YOUR FAVOURITE TUNES**

Music distracts the mind and induces a state of calmness.
It slows your heart rate and breathing, lowers blood pressure
and reduces the stress hormone noradrenaline associated
with insomnia. Take a moment to listen to some of your
favourite music today.

275. **SIP YOUR DRINK**

Taking sips of water or another drink regularly throughout
your meal can help you slow down and remember to chew
as you eat. A bonus is you'll get extra hydration and fill
up faster. What are you drinking today? **Darya**

276. **AN ACTIVITY THAT BRINGS JOY**

Sometimes exercise can feel like a drag! It can seem big, scary and time-consuming – difficult to even get started. So today, make movement a happy thing and do something that brings you joy. What activity is the most joyful for you? **Jamie S**

277. **BALL GAMES**

Since you were a child, have you ever just grabbed a ball and played catch? Today, find a ball or make a ball. Scrunch up a piece of paper and throw it around in the office with your colleagues, play catch with your kids or make several and try to juggle them on your own. **Dani**

278. **READ A SUMMARY OF TODAY'S NEWS**

Expanding our awareness of current affairs helps us to gain
perspective beyond our own lives. Today, read a summary
of the news. What stands out? What makes you think?

279. **A PRESENT YOU WANT**

At some point during this year it will be your birthday,
and whether you're a fan of birthdays or not, it's a good
day to pause and reflect. This year, focus on yourself –
decide one thing you will do for you. Get yourself a present
no one knows you want, book in some 'me' time, or treat
yourself to something.

280. **SORT YOUR POST**

Take a moment when you pick up your post to toss out all
the junk and to open routine items. You'll be surprised how
manageable that stack of letters becomes if you throw flyers,
adverts and unwanted magazines away immediately.
Caroline

281. **MOVE IN A NEW WAY**

Whether you take a class, have a dance or go for a walk, hike,
jog, bike ride, skate or roller skate – moving doesn't have to
be about pain and sweat. The more variety the better for your
body, and you won't get bored. Today, pick something active
you've not tried before and move in a new way. **Jamie S**

282. **CONSIDER THE DAY AHEAD**

Either you run the day or the day runs you. Sit down for
a moment and walk through your day. What is important?
What is not? What do you want to achieve? Then do it.

Make a plan here:

....

....

....

.

....

....

....

....

....

....

283. **CELEBRATE SALAD**

Make salad part of a meal today or, even better, the main
event. The possibilities are endless: warm, cold, chopped,
shaved, leafy, meaty, hearty, light . . . I could go on!
Have fun mixing up flavours, textures and great combos.
You might go for a hearty main, a sexy side salad or
a killer sandwich filling. Over to you. **Jamie**

284. **END OF WEEK PREP FOR NEXT WEEK**

What's one thing you can do at the end of this week that's going to make Monday easier? Fill the car up with petrol? Iron an outfit ready for work? Get a load of washing done? Stock up on lunch items? Think of one thing that trips you up on Monday morning and prepare for it early. You'll enjoy the weekend more and you'll have more energy next week if you take care of it in advance. **Caroline**

285. **DIM THE LIGHTS**

Optimize your environment for mindful eating by lighting a candle or dimming the lights. Research has shown you eat faster under bright light, so set the mood and enjoy the change of pace. **Darya**

286. **BEST PART OF YOUR DAY**

Mindfulness is often about being present in small moments.
Today, capture a moment that you enjoyed, however
simple, and record it here:

....

....

....

....

....

....

....

....

....

....

287.
REFLECT
AND
RENEW

Throughout the course of this book, you've hopefully been forming some sustainable habits that will last you the rest of your life.

Make a list of the things that have become a habit and celebrate them!

LOVE

288. **ACCEPT YOURSELF**

Such a cliché, but it's true: you are the most important person
in your life. Accept yourself with all your quirks and 'flaws'
today. Do something to treat yourself – you deserve it.

289. **RECALL SOMETHING FUNNY**

Overwhelming day? Do you have a lot on your plate right now? Remembering fun things tickles the pleasure centre of the brain and helps you relax. So recall a fun memory, a good joke or something that made you smile.

290. **TAKE CARE OF YOURSELF**

Neglecting personal needs can impact physical and mental wellbeing, and putting off scheduling appointments creates low-level anxiety that can dampen your productivity. Schedule an appointment with a doctor, dentist, accountant or neglected friend. You'll feel more relaxed immediately and it only takes a phone call. **Caroline**

291. **TAKE A MOMENT IN NATURE**

Today, take a moment to go out and enjoy nature.
Do you see budding spring flowers? Or the first signs
of autumn? Just five minutes of active time outside is
good for your mood and self-esteem, so get out there.

292. **ORGANIZE YOUR CLOTHES FOR TOMORROW**

Lay out what you will wear tomorrow, right down to the tie,
tights, earrings or cufflinks. Get it done early, before you are
so wiped out that you can't be bothered. You'll sleep better
and longer knowing that you won't be hunting down a shoe
or hastily redressing when you discover too late that you're
missing a button or that your shirt has a stain. **Caroline**

293. **SOMETHING TO LOOK FORWARD TO**

Anticipating future fun is an easy way to improve your
mood and broaden your perspective from the daily routine.
Put on your adventure hat and plan a getaway, a special
event, a night out or an exciting change in your life.
What are you looking forward to?

294. **CLEAR OUT FIVE ITEMS**

Reorganizing your desk, kitchen, files and clothes drawers
is usually on everyone's to-do list but seldom gets addressed.
Half the battle is weeding out items of minimal (or negative)
utility. Open a drawer today and challenge yourself to get
rid of at least five things. **Caroline**

MIND

295. DO A TASK YOU'VE BEEN PUTTING OFF

Select one task languishing on your to-do list. Pick up that extension lead at the DIY shop, change the hard-to-reach light bulb in that cupboard, call an elderly relative, make an appointment to get your teeth checked. Just pick one thing from your nagging to-do list and get it done today. **Caroline**

296. RE-DO A FAVOURITE MICRO-ACTION

Browse back through past micro-actions and choose one which you've found especially enjoyable. Reflect on why you found it particularly good or fun for you. Re-do it again today.

297. CUDDLE AN ANIMAL

Time spent with animals is a guaranteed happiness boost – hospitals and nursing homes often practise animal therapy for precisely this reason. Being with our furry friends simply gives us a feeling of wellbeing. So cuddle your pet, your neighbour's cat or take a walk to the nearest park to get your dose of animal love.

298. **DO YOUR BIT TO SAVE WATER**

Have your daily dose to drink, but also do one small micro-action to reduce your water consumption. Fix a leak, turn off the tap while brushing your teeth, use less water for the dishes, don't dwell in the shower. You can also save water in less obvious ways. Did you know that 10 litres of water are used to make one sheet of paper and 91 litres are used to make 0.5kg of plastic? Could you cut some out from your life?

299. **TAKE THE STAIRS AFTER LUNCH**

After your lunch today, climb a flight or two of stairs. Instead of taking the lift back to your office, walk up part of the way. If you ate at your desk, walk down a flight or two and then come back. Simple exertion will help jump-start your metabolism just when digestion is slowing it down and help you have a productive afternoon. **Caroline**

300. **ENJOY A SMALL ACHIEVEMENT**

Research has shown that it's small, frequent boosts of joy
that lead to happiness, not the rare big stuff. It's the little
things in daily life that have the power to make lasting
improvements to our happiness. So celebrate a small
achievement today – having your favourite lunch, moving
for just five minutes, choosing a book instead of your
iPad or receiving a smile from someone you like.

301. **A MAN YOU LOOK UP TO**

Today, consider which man in your life you look up to and
why. Is it your dad, grandfather, friend, neighbour, a teacher
or someone else who has left a positive mark on your life?
Reflect on him today.

FOOD

302. **FISH MISSION**

Try a fish you've never had before. There are so many species of fish out there, yet we tend to stick to just a handful of varieties. In the UK, it's usually cod, haddock, salmon and tuna. They may be delicious, but there are loads of alternatives and choosing a different fish not only means we can help relieve overfished and threatened species, but also that we discover new flavours to fall in love with. Speak to your fishmonger, see what they recommend and go fish! Choose responsibly sourced options, if you can. **Jamie**

303. **DANCE LIKE NO ONE'S WATCHING**

Moving your body is an incredible thing, especially when you can rock it to your favourite tunes. So get moving today – be it in the car, on your way to work, at home or in the office. Turn it up and dance for the entire song! **Dani**

304. **PICK UP A CLASSIC**

Books have the unique ability to take us on a journey through space, time, perspective and reality. The classics may feel dry and antiquated, but they have stood the test of time and can be surprisingly relevant to us now, even when written hundreds of years ago. Pick up a classic book you want to read or have read before and loved – and see where it takes you.

305. **HANDY HYDRATION**

Today, keep water handy. I've talked about it before, but it's important to repeat to get into the habit. Two-thirds of our bodies are made up of water, so if you're not hydrated, you're not at your best. Wherever you are, make it easy to stay topped up with humble H_2O. Stash a bottle in your bag, keep a glass topped up at your desk and pop a jug on the dinner table. The beauty of water is that it's so simple and cheap to hydrate – all you have to do is turn on the tap. Bottoms up! **Jamie**

306. **GO BAREFOOT**

We spend so much time in socks or shoes. Today, take
yours off and go barefoot, even just at home. For the best
experience, go outside and walk on fresh grass, and really
feel the ground under the soles of your feet.

307. **LIGHT A CANDLE**

Candles are magical and powerful things. They bring light
to the darkness, warmth to the cold. Light a candle today
and remember a loved one, celebrate a special day,
have a moment of quietness or simply just enjoy the
soft atmosphere it creates.

308. **WALK, EVERY HOUR, ON THE HOUR**

Have a day when you set your alarm to ring every hour.
When the alarm goes off, get up and walk around. No need
to make it a long walk; even just around the room is enough
to be beneficial. **Jamie S**

309. **MAKE A BETTER CHOICE**

Make one choice a better one. We make thousands of
choices every day, and research says we're unconscious
of as many as 60% of those. We run on autopilot and repeat
the same things from one day to the next. So it's really the
small changes we can make here and there that truly make a
difference. So make a better choice. Today, have a healthier
breakfast, put your running gear out in the evening to get
you motivated in the morning, spend some time outside,
or work standing up for a bit.

310. **WRITE DOWN A THOUGHT**

What's one thing you have on your mind right now? Is it an undone task that keeps bugging you? A nice event you're looking forward to? A feeling you have but cannot fully comprehend or express? Writing it down focuses your thinking. This can also give your mind a rest and the thing itself a bit more perspective. So pick up your pen and do your best to express it in words here:

....

....

....

....

....

....

....

....

311. **DAILY DAIRY**

Unless you're a vegan or intolerant, dairy is an important part of our diet. Make sure you include a little bit of dairy in a meal today. As well as being a great source of calcium and vitamin A, dairy foods are also packed with protein, which is essential for growth and repair. It's true that some dairy products are also high in fat but, enjoyed in moderation, they have many benefits. Try adding a dollop of yoghurt to a meal, finishing a dish with a grating of Parmesan or embracing naturally lower-fat cheese choices such as feta, ricotta and cottage cheese. **Jamie**

312. **DON'T SUPERSIZE**

Portion control for many of us has gone crazy. We're all guilty of sometimes going back for seconds (even thirds!) or happily devouring a large portion just because we're offered one. Today, pay attention when you portion up your food. Don't pile your plate too high and be mindful of recommended serving sizes for things like pasta and rice – it sounds obvious, but if you measure it out before cooking, there'll be no leftovers to tempt you! **Jamie**

313. **TALK TO AN OLDER PERSON**

We often get caught in the here and now. As we grow older
we start seeing the patterns and the deeper meaning in life.
Gain perspective early – talk to an older person today.

314. **SHORTEN YOUR MEETINGS**

End hour-long meetings at 50 minutes, half hour ones at 25.
If it's not your meeting, help it to end promptly once its purpose
has been accomplished. That extra ten minutes in every hour
will be a productivity boost for everyone involved.
Meeting adjourned. **Caroline**

315. **WRITE DOWN WHAT HAPPENED TODAY**

In the evening our brain is overloaded with stimuli from the day, which can make it hard to relax. Take a moment to write down the things on your mind from today. Then forget about them for tonight and have some downtime.

....

....

....

....

....

....

....

....

FOOD

316. **BUILD UP AN APPETITE**

There's nothing like sitting down at the table with a big appetite, ready to tuck in. Those amazing smells that make your mouth water and the feeling of satisfaction after a well-earned meal are hard to beat. Today, make an effort to build up an appetite, whether that means avoiding grazing, getting outside and active before sitting down, or simply waiting until you're truly hungry before you have a meal. **Jamie**

317.
**REFLECT
AND
RENEW**

We are nearing the end of this book and you've
now done more than 300 micro-actions for
a happier, healthier you.

Take a moment to look through your notes and start
forming a story of the person you are becoming.
Then share that story with someone – a friend,
partner or family member. No doubt they'll be
happy to take part in it and help you forward.

318. **MOVE TOGETHER**

Moving together keeps you more accountable and makes
it more fun. Team up with a friend for a light jog in the park,
schedule a joint workout with your significant other, or join
a group class. If you have kids, make your joint time active –
go walking, skating, surfing, cycling or visit the park.

319. **DO SOME PEOPLE WATCHING**

Every person who walks past you on the street or sits on the
same bus as you has their own story. They have their dreams,
fears, insecurities, victories, strengths, reasons to smile and
reasons to cry. Sit down today in a place with people around
you and do some people watching. Try to construct the stories
of those you see – their backgrounds, professions, highs
and lows. It can really change the way you look at others.

320. **LEARN ONE THING ABOUT HOW YOUR BODY WORKS**

Knowing how the body works is key to making it work better for you. So open a dictionary, a book, or browse reliable websites and read something about the human body. What interesting fact can you find that helps you treat your body better?

321. **SPEND LESS ON SOMETHING**

Saving money depends as much upon small daily behaviours as conscious financial goal setting. Small spending decisions on coffees, bottled water, magazines, lunch, toys, taxi rides and fancy cocktails invisibly raise our daily expenses until we run short or compromise our financial goals. Pick a situation and choose the less expensive choice: make your lunch, walk instead of taking the bus or sip a glass of water instead of a martini. If you can make small cuts here and there, your wallet will thank you very soon. **Caroline**

FOOD

322. **NATURALLY SWEET**

Whether you have a sweet tooth or not, sugar usually plays a part in our day-to-day diets. We all know too much is bad for us so minimize your processed-sugar intake today by sweetening your food and drinks with something natural. Try adding fruit to your breakfast instead of sugar, or using fresh fruit to flavour water rather than choosing a sugary drink. **Jamie**

323. **YOUR GROWTH MOMENT**

Today, recall a moment of growth in your life. How has it changed you or improved things for you? What did you learn?

Write it here:

....

....

....

....

....

....

....

....

....

....

324. **SOMETHING YOU ALWAYS WANTED TO ASK**

Children ask questions all the time. Often they ask questions we have never thought of, and we learn something new in the process. Today, ask a question you always wanted to know the answer to – you might be surprised at the answer.

325. **DO ONE THING DIFFERENTLY**

Routines and habits are comfortable and often desired. So challenge yourself once in a while. Change one thing. It might be big or small, related to moving, eating, yourself or the people you care about. Doing that one thing differently will stimulate your brain in new ways.

326. **CHILDHOOD FUN**

Do you remember finding sincere joy in the plainest and simplest of things when you were younger? Boost your mood today and do one thing you really enjoyed as a child.

327. **ORGANIZE YOUR WARDROBE IN FIVE MINUTES**

With a timer set for five minutes, see how many items you can pull together in your wardrobe to make it easier to find what you need. In this time, can you hang all your tops/shirts together in a group, line your shoes together in pairs or remove any old plastic wrap and wire hangers from the rail? You can accomplish a lot in five minutes, and your next encounter with your wardrobe will be more swift and satisfying. **Caroline**

328. **REARRANGE A ROOM**

Do you dream about a complete room makeover but never quite achieve it? Making just one or two positive alterations can give you a real lift and inspire you to change it up whenever you've got ten minutes to spare. Move a lamp, hang a picture . . . and wouldn't that chair be better by the window? It's fun, it's fast and it lasts. **Caroline**

329. **A WEAKNESS OF YOURS**

What is one weakness you have? Try to identify something you honestly want to work on and apply the 'strength-based' approach to it. How can you use a strength you have to help you improve on your weakness? For example, can you use your strength in planning to overcome your shyness in social situations?

330. **MAKE A RESOLUTION FOR TODAY**

When you make a specific resolution you are up to ten times
more likely to keep it than if you have an unspecific goal.
Go ahead: make a resolution for something you will
do or achieve today and write it here:

....

....

....

....

....

....

....

....

....

....

FOOD

331. **GO THE WHOLE WAY**

I've challenged you on this before. Quite simply, if you
swap out white refined bread, pasta, rice or noodles for the
wholewheat or wholemeal alternatives, it could be the easiest
but biggest, most positive change you make to your diet this
year. You'll get more depth of flavour, and as they're packed
with fibre they'll keep you feeling fuller for longer, as well
as helping to lower blood cholesterol. **Jamie**

332. **FIND A NEW PLACE**

Today, take a mindful walk around your neighbourhood and find a new spot. Most days we walk the same streets and visit the same places but do not really pay attention. Today, pick up your coffee from somewhere else, have lunch in a different location, pop into that bookshop you always wanted to visit or walk down a new road in your neighbourhood or path out in the countryside. You may discover a new favourite place.

333. **GO CUPBOARD SHOPPING**

We've all got those shadowy kitchen shelves filled with tins and odds and sods. This micro-action is super simple. Root around in a kitchen cupboard and use up one ingredient rather than buying a duplicate you don't need. Next time you go shopping to stock up on new items, check your cupboards first for forgotten-about ingredients. We often fill our shopping trolleys with things we already have, so you'll save waste and money – and you may even uncover a tasty surprise! **Jamie**

334. **MICRO-HELP SOMEONE**

Today, micro-help someone else. Do a small deed,
show gratitude, say 'thank you', offer a helping hand –
it'll be more than worth it.

335. **WANDER AROUND**

For today's lunch (or coffee break) have a wander. Leave
the house or workplace and meander around the same way
you would if you were on vacation in a new place. Stroll
through the little park a few blocks away, window shop or
browse in a bookstore. Research shows that environmental
stimulation helps us to maintain focus and mental energy.
Fifteen minutes will do the trick! **Caroline**

336. **CALCULATE SOMETHING IN YOUR HEAD**

Remember when you learned the multiplication tables by heart in school? How well can you do it now? Calculating simple things in your head is a skill you easily lose if you don't practise it. Have a go and do some mental arithmetic today.

337. **TWO-MINUTE WORKOUT: BALANCE!**

Proprioception (difficult word, I know!) is the body's ability to know its own position. Cues from the environment, your feet, inner ear and eyes tell your body which muscles to use. Good balance means better coordination and posture. To train your balance, practise standing on one leg for two minutes. **Jamie S**

338. **WHAT MAKES YOU PROUD?**

What lifts your spirits? It could be something you did,
that someone else did or something that you just think
is awesome in the world. Being able to enjoy the
'small things' will enable you to think positive.

Note them down here:

....

....

....

....

....

....

....

....

....

339. **YOUR FAVOURITE MICRO-ACTION**

It's again time to reflect on a favourite micro-action of yours
and repeat it. Browse back through the book – which
micro-action has had a big impact on you? Repeat it!

340. **WASH FINGERPRINTS OFF A WALL**

Arm yourself with a soapy sponge or a spray cleaner and
pick a wall or windowsill that needs attention, then go at it.
You'll be surprised at how gratifying the result of five minutes'
labour can be. Try the areas around light switches for speedy
satisfaction – they often get a bit grimy but clean up fast.
Caroline

341. **PUT ONE THING IN ITS PLACE**

Start the day organized. Choose one thing to pick up and put in its place. Be it work papers, a pile of clothes or the children's toys – you've already achieved one good thing today.

342. **CARRY YOUR WEIGHT**

At the supermarket? Pick a basket instead of a trolley or, even better, leave the car at home and walk to the shops and carry your shopping bag. Muscles will have to work harder to carry extra weight, which in turn will boost your metabolism, strength, circulation, improve core muscles and give your whole body a workout. **Jamie S**

343. **HELP SOMEONE OUT**

Who could you help today? We've all had those occasions in the past when someone has reached out a helping hand to us at the right moment. In many cases the feeling of helping, of giving without the need to get something in return, is an even better one. Provide a little help to someone today – a friend, neighbour, colleague or a stranger on the street.

344. **SCHEDULE 'ME' TIME**

Today, consciously put aside a bit of time for yourself. Many of us spend a lot of our time catering to other people's needs or doing what is expected of us. What would you do today if you could do anything, just for you? Schedule it in and take that time.

....

....

345. **READ SOMETHING POETIC**

Today, pick up a book or a poem and immerse yourself in it for a moment. Whether you enjoy poetry or not, reading it is one of the best ways to focus and stimulate your brain. Poetry is an unexplored area for many, but the right poem really can whisk you away to another world.

346. **EXPLORE THE NEIGHBOURHOOD**

Put on your walking shoes and go out to explore your surroundings. Notice something new. Find a place you haven't visited before. Admire something a second longer. When you are paying attention to what's around you and get lost in the moment you may not only experience something new but also end up walking that extra mile.

347.
REFLECT
AND
RENEW

For this review – take a moment and look
back on your journey so far.

What changes are you seeing in yourself?

In what situations are you feeling the happiest,
most accomplished, most self-assured?

How can you strengthen this feeling in yourself?

348: **VEGGIE BREKKIE**

Mix things up today and incorporate a veg element into your brekkie. Variety is key for a healthy diet, and if you can get one of your five-a-day portions in your first meal, then you'll be off to a great start! Think creamy avocado on toast, fluffy sweetcorn pancakes, a refreshing green smoothie or a veg-packed omelette. **Jamie**

349. **CLEAR OUT YOUR UNDERWEAR DRAWER**

Nothing gets worn and washed as much as underwear, and there's a tendency to add new to old without really tossing out the truly tatty unmentionables. Take a moment to toss out hole-y and unpaired socks, greyed-out vests and elastic-less pants. Even undercover, worn-out undies are a downer. **Caroline**

350. **REACH FOR THE FURTHEST PACKET**

Save on food waste – and hopefully save yourself a bit of cash too. Reach to the back of one of your lesser-used cupboards and pick out a tin or packet to use up in a meal. Even though store-cupboard items may feel like they last for ever, you'll be surprised how many we let expire hiding away at the back. **Jamie**

351. **WHO INSPIRES YOU?**

It is human nature to search for answers to life's big questions, and many of us do so by seeking inspiration from wise women and men, past and present. Who is that person who inspires you, makes you think and, above all, would make you act? Alive or long gone, famous or known by few, a specific person or a group, think about how they inspire you today.

352. **PAUSE YOUR MOVEMENT**

Next time you're up and moving, pause your movement for just two minutes. Moving your body everyday is paramount but so is taking breaks – it's when your muscles rest and develop and it can really put you in touch with how your body is feeling. How could you stop moving for two minutes? Cool down after a workout, listen to a song or take a stretching break. Or simply find a space where you can sit or lie down and allow your body to relax. **Dani**

353. **REARRANGE YOUR WALLET**

Wallet full of old receipts? Still have foreign currency rattling around from your holiday nine months ago? How about all those business cards you intended to enter as contacts? Take five minutes today to rearrange your wallet: remove old papers, make the most important cards easily accessible and get rid of change. You'll be surprised how much more rapid and stress-free your daily transactions will be after just a few small changes. **Caroline**

354. **PUT OUT YOUR WORKOUT CLOTHES**

A morning workout is a great habit to get into, but it can be really hard to get started. A simple way to give you that extra push is to lay out your exercise clothes right next to your bed the night before. It'll feel easier and more motivating in the morning for sure.

355. **BEST OF THE YEAR**

Introspective thinking and writing can have numerous health benefits. Today, look back at the past year. What do you recall? What was the best, coolest, funniest, most memorable part of the year gone by? Was there something that you really loved?

Take a moment to record it here:

....

....

....

....

....

....

....

....

356. **ONE NEW FOOD SKILL**

Whether you teach yourself or someone else – get in the kitchen, try something new and teach one food skill today. Learning a food skill is powerful and will stick with you for life, especially for kids, so if you have little ones in your life teach them something simple, such as how to make a salad dressing. Maybe you've always wanted to learn how to get your poached eggs perfect or de-vein a juicy prawn. Whatever it is, give it a go! **Jamie**

357. **WHAT MATTERS MORE THAN MONEY?**

Reflect on one thing that is more important to you than money. Money for many of us is important and can bring lots of opportunities. But if you think money will bring happiness, think again. Money is good, but many other things are better. If you had no wealth (or all the wealth in the world) what would matter most to you?

358. **SEND SNAIL MAIL**

In this day of electronic everything we rarely anymore turn to traditional 'snail mail' (except for paper ads and bills). Today, make the postman happy and send someone a letter or a post card via traditional mail routes. Get a kick from imagining the joy and surprise of the person at the other end receiving your note!

359. **MORNING GLORY**

Whether you're a morning person or not, what happens in the first hour after waking up can have an immense impact on the rest of your day. Look back to micro-action 72: Modify One Morning Habit. What did you decide to change back then? If you're still sticking to it, maybe it's time to add another positive change. And if you're not sticking to it, try again or attempt a different one. Is eating breakfast your weak spot? Are you perpetually late in the morning? What could make your mornings go smoother?

360. **WHAT MAKES YOU ANGRY?**

Anger is powerful. Anger can trigger the body's 'fight or flight'
response and be bad for your health, so it's a good idea to let
off steam. What's a problem you'd like to get fixed in the world –
and how? Spend a few moments writing down what makes
your blood boil. Then take a deep breath and let it go . . .

....

....

....

....

....

....

....

....

361. **ENJOY GOOD MOOD FOOD**

Comforting food can make us feel all kinds of good,
so today enjoy a comfort food that makes you feel good.
Whether you're cooking it yourself or decamping elsewhere
to be cooked for, it's a great opportunity to get together
with friends and family and create a good mood meal
to share with the people you love. **Jamie**

362. **A MEMORY TO CHERISH**

What's a memory you recall and cherish from your early years?
Recalling good memories is not just nice, it's also been proven
to boost your overall happiness. So take a trip down memory
lane and relive those moments!

363. **ENJOY THE MOMENT**

We tend to rush through routines, chores and to-dos, always
focusing on the next thing on our agenda. This can be good for
getting things done, but we run the risk of forgetting to enjoy
the moment. So today, pause and be present in what you're
doing. It could be taking time over your morning tea or coffee,
finding something funny or relaxing with your feet up in the
evening. What moment will you fully enjoy today?

364. PLAN THE YEAR AHEAD

Although we are almost at the end of this book, it's simply the beginning of something new. Take a moment and write down your plans and objectives for the next year. What do you want to achieve? What do you want to learn? What do you want to improve in yourself? Make a short list and a plan for how you'll do it!

....

....

....

....

....

....

....

....

....

365. **YOU**

Congratulations! You've reached the final micro-action of this book. Now find a place in your bookshelf or bedroom where you can store this book to come back to when you need inspiration. Then set yourself a calendar reminder for a month or three from now, when you'll take an hour to just sit down and flip through the pages and reflect.

Thank you for this journey, and keep up being you.

YOU-APP IS DAILY MICRO-ACTIONS FOR A HAPPIER, HEALTHIER YOU

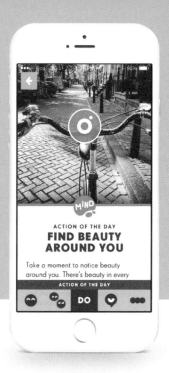

JOIN THE WORLD'S MOST POSITIVE COMMUNITY

Every day working on the YOU-app we get testimonials from people who have used the app and found micro-actions helpful. People cite being more mindful, more positive, making healthier choices, and understanding the power of small actions. Then at times there are longer, personal stories that just make us stop, and remind us why we do the work we do. This was one of those:

Dear YOU,

When I stumbled across YOU-app in January I was in a bad place in my life. I had lost my way and I was barely existing through each day. I had become a stranger to happiness – something completely unlike the 'me' I had always known.

I've found that my joy has come back through the daily actions, but in particular through my Keep It Up actions. I started out with the Read Something New micro-action which broke the monotony of reading for my studies. It reminded me that there is a whole world out there, which is the reason I'm putting myself through the slog of getting a degree at the ripe age of 39.

My next Keep It Up action was to Find Micro-Magic in Your Day. This helped me to find little moments of awe and gratitude each day, which I noticed became underlying awareness of gratitude throughout the day.

I moved on to taking 'me' time which is so important. I realise that now. The lack of downtime does take its toll. It's not easy as a homeschooling mum, coupled with minimal finances. I sometimes feel guilty, wanting time for myself. It makes me feel like a bad mother some days. But this action energised me and was so valuable.

I feel like the dip I went through last year was exactly that. Just a dip. Not an irreversible change. So thank you!

Toni

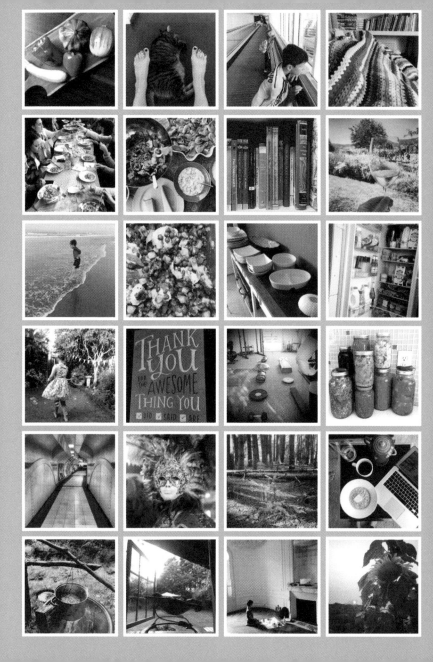

PENGUIN BOOKS

UK | USA | Canada | Ireland | Australia
India | New Zealand | South Africa

Penguin Books is part of the Penguin Random House
group of companies whose addresses can be found at
global.penguinrandomhouse.com.

Penguin
Random House
UK

First published 2015
001

Text copyright © Fifth Corner Inc., 2015

The moral right of the author has been asserted

Design by Smith & Gilmour

All images listed below © Jamie Oliver Enterprises Limited, 2006-2015
Actions 25, 53, 59, 82, 87, 93, 98, 105, 127, 150, 166, 170, 175, 184, 192,
213, 258, 275, 283, 302, 311, 322, 356, 361, photography: David Loftus
Actions 9, 42, 45, 58, 78, 111, 134, 141, 312, 331, photography: James Lyndsay
Actions 31, 43, 106, 117, photography: Sarah Tildesley
Action 37, photography: Matt Russell
Actions 66, 230, photography: Joe Sarah
Action 137, photography: Elspeth Meston
Action 199, photography: Dan Jones
Actions 151, 316, 348, photography: Jamie Oliver
Action 305, photography: Tara Fisher

With thanks to the following YOU-app users for their contributions:
BeeW, ChrisForestFood, cositas, divadiane, DocBells, GrahamEttridge,
HappyDaysNo.1, InternationalMenu, J_furr, JimmyCSmitz, Leap2itCate,
lindseyevans, livelittleadventures, Mamacha, mariastrat, NikNyg, Picasso,
rob7, spots_of_time, strawberry_girl, supersteph, twintasticand2more

Printed and bound in Italy by L.E.G.O. S.p.A.
A CIP catalogue record for this book is available from the British Library

ISBN: 978-1-405-92413-9

www.greenpenguin.co.uk